ANNYEONG?

A New Learning Paradigm rich in Culture and Stories

KOREAN!

2

ANNYEONG? KOREAN! _ Volume 2

First published in 2025 by Hello Korean Inc.
© 2025 Hyun Mi Kim, Jieun Kiaer and Nicola Fraschini

English Proofreading: **Gabriel Sparta**
Published by **Hur. Dae woo**
Marketing by **Hwang. Hyun kyung**
Designed by **Lee. Seung mi**
Character Design by **Lee. Jae yeop**

All rights reserved.
No part of this publication may be reproduced or transmitted in any form or by any means, electronic or mechanical, including photocopying, recording or any other information storage and retrieval system, without prior permission in writing from the publisher.

ISBN 979-11-992526-0-8 (13700)
Printed and bound in Republic of Korea by Hello Printec

AUTHORS

Hyun Mi Kim

Hyun Mi Kim has taught Korean to students in Canada, South Korea, the United States, and now Australia. Through her various teaching roles, she learned what students want by listening and connecting their interests with curriculum requirements. This dedication earned her the Citations for Outstanding Contributions to Student Learning from the University of Western Australia. Her rich experience enabled her to develop the Korean curriculum for the Western Australia Department of Education. Additionally, students' questions inspired her to co-author three books, including *Mission Accomplished Korean 1 & 2* (Hawoo, 2022/2023) and *Korean Conversation Gambits* (Routledge, 2024). She holds a B.A. in education and an M.A. in Korean culture from Ewha Womans University. Her cultural studies background leads her to believe that engaging students in Korean culture through language strengthens their connection to Korean society and enhances understanding. She feels that learning languages builds connections and friendships, cultivating hope for a brighter future.

Jieun Kiaer

Prof Jieun Kiaer is the YBM KF Professor of Korean Linguistics at the University of Oxford. She also serves as a Korean Consultant for the Oxford English Dictionary and is recognized as a leading expert in Korean linguistics and Hallyu (Korean Wave) studies. Prof Kiaer holds a PhD in Linguistics from King's College London, as well as an MA in Linguistics and a BA in Child and Family Studies from Seoul National University. Her innovative approaches to language learning include fandom language learning, AI-driven digital linguistics, and storytelling methods that integrate culture and personal interests.

Nicola Fraschini

Nicola Fraschini is a Senior Lecturer at the University of Melbourne, where he is director of the Global Korea Research Hub. His research interests are the psychology of language teaching and learning and Q methodology. He is co-author of the textbooks *Mission Accomplished: Korean 1 & 2* (Hawoo, 2022/2023), and co-editor of *Advancing Language Research through Q Methodology* (Multilingual Matters, 2024) and *Innovative Methods in Korean Language Teaching* (Routledge, 2025). In 2024, he was awarded from the Republic of Korea the Prime Minister's citation for his work supporting the Korean language.

FOREWORD

The Korean language is gaining momentum globally-not only through K-pop and K-dramas but through a growing desire to understand the country's culture, customs, and everyday life. In this second volume of *Annyeong? Korean!*, we continue our mission to make Korean language and culture accessible, inclusive, and truly engaging for learners around the world.

While traditional textbooks often focus heavily on grammar rules in isolation, Annyeong? Korean! offers something different: a learning journey grounded in culture, real places, and practical experience. Volume 2 of *Annyeong? Korean!* introduces real-life situations and culturally rich settings, from the DMZ to hanbok rentals near Gyeongbokgung Palace, and even a trip to Jeju Island with its legendary haenyeo. These scenarios are brought to life through a diverse cast of characters, interactive dialogues, and tasks that reflect how Korean is actually spoken and lived.

Volume 2 also helps learners navigate the nuances of Korean communication-from formal and informal speech to regional dialects and culture-specific expressions-essential for developing genuine fluency. With embedded media suggestions, cultural insights, and CEFR-aligned competencies, learners are guided step-by-step to communicate with confidence in authentic settings.

Whether you are a beginner building on your first steps or a teacher seeking an engaging, holistic curriculum, *Annyeong? Korean!* offers a sustainable and inspiring way to connect with Korea today. So, are you ready for the next step? 함께 떠나 볼까요? Let's explore the language and life of Korea-together.

The authors

CONTENT

Foreword	…	4
Content	…	5
Book structure	…	6
Unit structure	…	8
Characters	…	14

Unit 1.	I Am the King!	…	17
Unit 2.	Am I Your Friend?	…	33
Unit 3.	National Team Member	…	49
Unit 4.	Treasure No. 1: The Light Stick	…	65
Unit 5.	Take Care Not to Catch a Cold!	…	79
Unit 6.	Magpie's Seollal…	…	93
Unit 7.	DMZ Café	…	107
Unit 8.	The King of Tteokbokki Reviewers	…	121
Unit 9.	Let's Go	…	137
Unit 10.	The Sea and the Haenyeo's Breath	…	151

Appendices

Irregular Conjugations	…	166
Formal and Informal Language	…	168
Word List (Korean to English, by unit)	…	170
Word List (Korean to English)	…	176
Word List (English to Korean)	…	182
Answers to Exercises	…	189
Dialogue, Listening Transcripts, and Translations	…	192

STRUCTURE

Unit	Title	Vocabulary and Expressions	Grammar	Dialogue
1	I Am the King!	Clothes and dresses	–(으)ㄹ 거예요; –(으)ㄹ 수 있다	Sarang and Sophia visit an hanbok rental shop
2	Am I Your Friend?	Working life	반말; 보다; 제일	Umid talks with a colleague
3	National Team Member	Leisure activities	–아/어야 하다; –고; 하고,	Sam seeks advise from Priya about visiting a ski resort
4	Treasure No. 1: The Light Stick	Personal interests and fandom	–습니다; –지만	Haru arrives at the entrance of a concert hall
5	Take Care Not to Catch a Cold!	Illness and medicines	–아/어서(이유); –(으)ㄴ 후에	Maduka is unwell and visits a clinic
6	Magpie's Seollal…	Holidays and festivities	–(으)려고; –거나; (이)나	Sarang and Caroline discuss their plans for the Lunar New Year festivities
7	DMZ Café	South and North Korea	–(으)ㄹ까요?(추측); – 지요?; 도	Maduka and Gabriel discuss to visit the DMZ
8	The King of Tteokbokki Reviewers	Street food and food delivery	–기 전에; –아/어서(순차); 에게/한테; 에게서/한테서	Maduka and Tao discuss a YouTube video
9	Let's Go!	Sport events and personality	–(으)니까(이유); –고 있다	Tao and Van Binh decide to watch a baseball game
10	The Sea and the Haenyeo's Breath	Sustainable work activities	–지 않다; – 지 못하다; –으려고+동사	Sarang and Caroline meet Sarang's grandmother, a haenyeo

Reading	Listening	Activity	Culture
Visitor information	Sophia's Vlog	Activities at the Korean royal palaces	The Korean traditional dress in the 21C
Text messages between co-workers	Sarang and Umid discuss slips-of-the-tongue in Korean	Describing one's past slip-of-the-tongue	Formal and informal language
Safety guidelines of a ski resort	Sam and his friend ask for information about transportation	Suggesting places to visit	Winter sports in Korea
Article on the daily routine of K-pop idols	Haru and Caroline listen to an announcements at a music concert	Understanding announcements in public spaces	K-pop concerts and light sticks
Short story in an essay magazine	Sarang is unwell and explains the symptoms to a doctor	Filling out a clinic registration card	Korean healthcare system
Blog entry about Buddhist Templestay	Umid and Sam listen to a news report	Explaining one's country holidays	Calling one's relatives in Korean
Newsletter entry	Maduka and Gabriel approaches the ticket office	Using and online booking system	A new café near North Korea
YouTube video comments	Tao listen to a podcast about soul food	Telling about one's soul food	Koreans' comfort food
Interview to a baseball fan	A baseball player answer to a Q&A radio session	Conducting an interview about hobbies and personality	Korean sport crowd culture
Statistics about Jeju island and haenyeo	Caroline listens to a public lecture about haenyeo	Talking about haenyeo's life	Korean female divers

Book structure 07

UNIT STRUCTURE

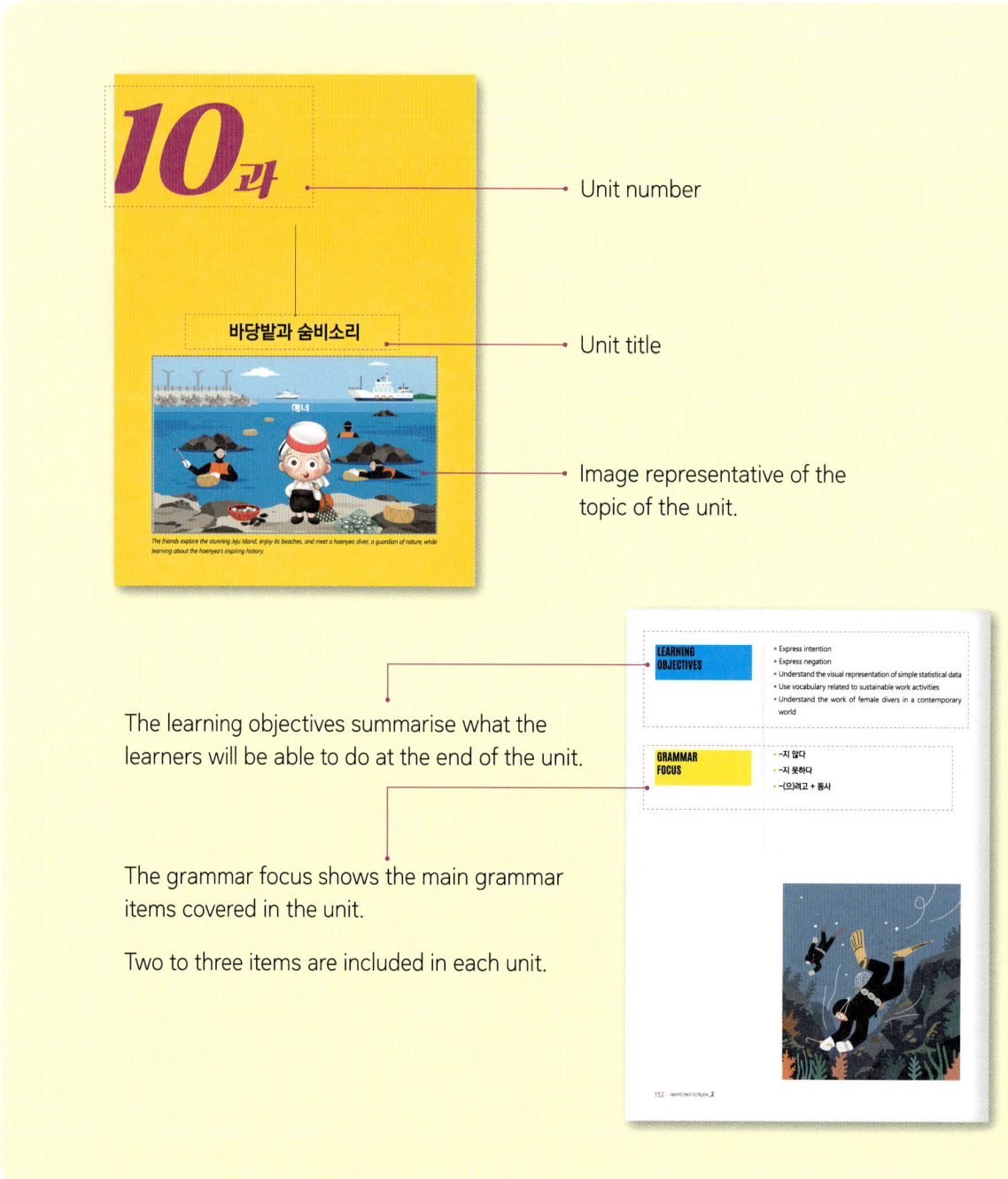

Unit number

Unit title

Image representative of the topic of the unit.

The learning objectives summarise what the learners will be able to do at the end of the unit.

The grammar focus shows the main grammar items covered in the unit.

Two to three items are included in each unit.

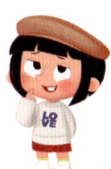

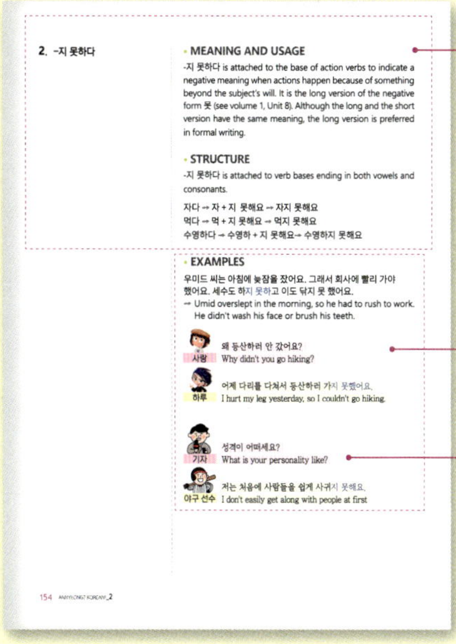

2. -지 못하다

· MEANING AND USAGE

-지 못하다 is attached to the base of action verbs to indicate a negative meaning when actions happen because of something beyond the subject's will. It is the long version of the negative form 못 (see volume 1, Unit 8). Although the long and the short version have the same meaning, the long version is preferred in formal writing.

· STRUCTURE

-지 못하다 is attached to verb bases ending in both vowels and consonants.

자다 → 자 + 지 못해요 → 자지 못해요
먹다 → 먹 + 지 못해요 → 먹지 못해요
수영하다 → 수영하 + 지 못해요→ 수영하지 못해요

· EXAMPLES

우미드 씨는 아침에 늦잠을 잤어요. 그래서 회사에 빨리 가야 했어요. 세수도 하지 못하고 이도 닦지 못 했어요.
→ Umid overslept in the morning, so he had to rush to work. He didn't wash his face or brush his teeth.

사랑 왜 등산하러 안 갔어요? Why didn't you go hiking?
하루 어제 다리를 다쳐서 등산하러 가지 못했어요. I hurt my leg yesterday, so I couldn't go hiking.

기자 성격이 어떠세요? What is your personality like?
야구 선수 저는 처음에 사람들을 쉽게 사귀지 못해요. I don't easily get along with people at first

154 ANNYEONG? KOREAN!_2

Each grammar item is introduced first by an explanation of its meaning and usage, then by an illustration of its structure.

Plenty of examples are provided so the learner can fully understand how a grammar item is used.

Dialogues are provided so that learners can see how the grammar item is used in context.

A dialogue provides the students with the opportunity to practice oral communication, giving a real-life context.

Each dialogue is followed by a role-play exercise. Students therefore can safely practice the main grammar items guided by the structure of the dialogue.

The role-play also provides the students with new vocabulary to learn.

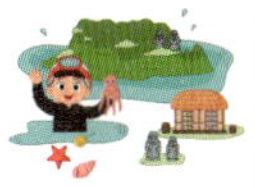

대화 DIALOGUE

Sarang and Caroline went down to the shore to say hello to Sarang's grandmother, Seondeok, who works as a haenyeo. 10-1

선덕 할머니 바다까지 왜 나왔어? 집에서 기다리지?
사랑 캐롤라인 씨가 해녀에 관심이 많아서 할머니 보러 같이 왔어요.
캐롤라인 안녕하세요?
선덕 할머니 그래요. 잘 왔어요.
캐롤라인 어… 할머님, 해녀 일이 힘들지 않으세요?
선덕 할머니 아니요. 즐거워요.

Role-play the dialogue by substituting the colour-coded words or phrases with the prompts below.

해녀 일이 힘들다 - 아니요. 즐거워요.
춥다 - 네. 안 추워요.
어린 해산물을 잡다 - 네. 안 잡아요.
혼자 일하다 - 네. 혼자 일 안 해요.
해산물을 한꺼번에 많이 잡다 - 네. 많이 안 잡아요.

156 ANNYEONG? KOREAN!_2

UNIT STRUCTURE

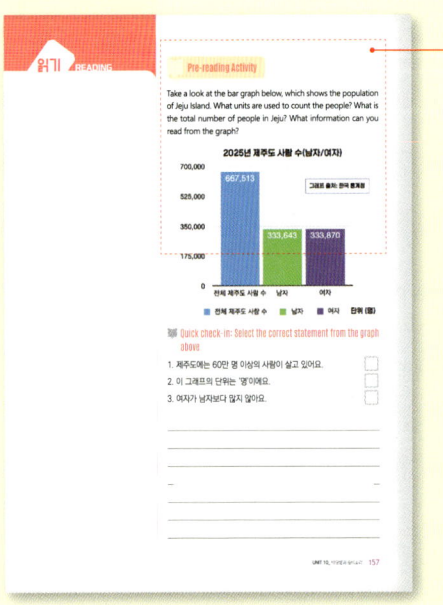

Reading activities are structured into three parts. In the pre-reading activity, learners practice vocabulary and expressions necessary to understand the reading fully.

In the reading activity, learners approach the main material. The material for the reading activities varies in format from unit to unit, spanning official websites, newsletters, YouTube comments, an easy magazine, and statistics, providing students with an opportunity to approach the language used in different contexts.

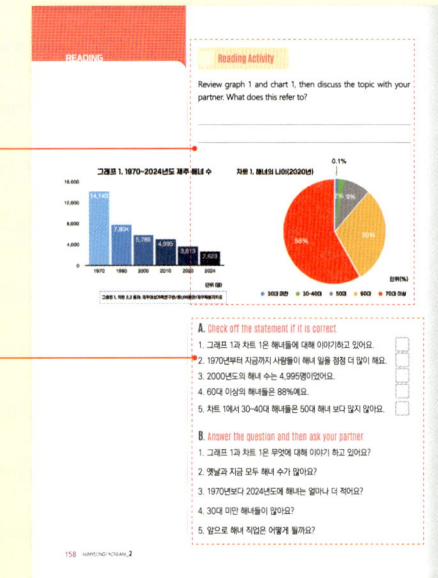

After each reading, the learners can check their understanding of the content through True/False styles quizzes and open ended questions.

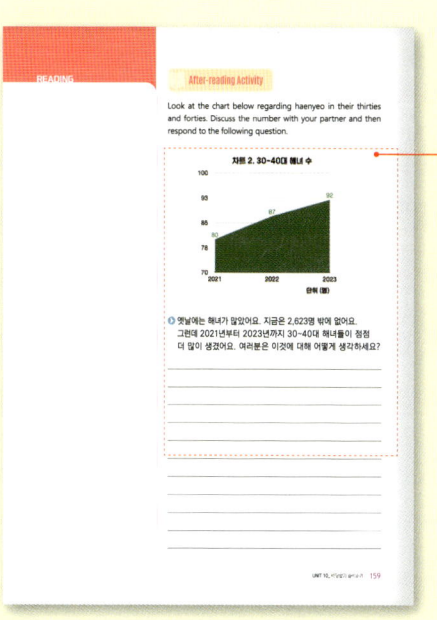

A follow-up reading activity provides the opportunity to expand the communicative settings, by using the content learned in either a written or an oral activity.

Each listening activity is introduced by an exercises through which learners can get used to the main vocabulary and expressions used in the main listening.

Them main listening is always introduced by a listening question, i.e. what the learners should focus their attention when listening to the recording.

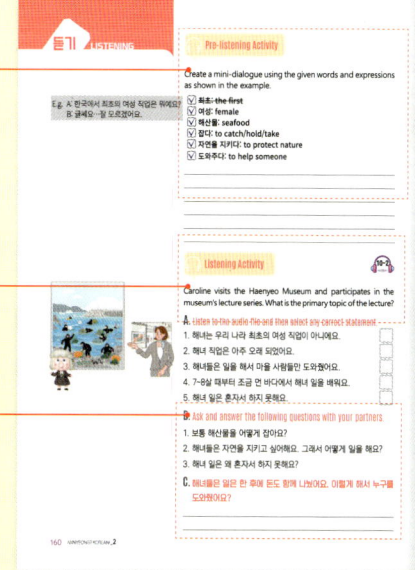

At the end of the listening activity, the learners will find an exercise they can use to check their comprehension.

Unit structure 11

UNIT STRUCTURE

At the end of the main listening activity, the learners have the opportunity to practice the language learned in the unit in a real-life like activity.

A K-culture corner introduces the learners to an aspect of contemporary Korean culture and society mentioned in the unit.

A K-media corner provides suggestions to the learners for films, dramas, and fiction works through which they can observe and experience the main cultural aspects included in the subject. Through these suggestions, learners can also maximise their language exposure.

The learners can also get used to real expressions that they may hear in Korea.

At the end of each unit, the learners can reflect on their learning through a reflective sheet.

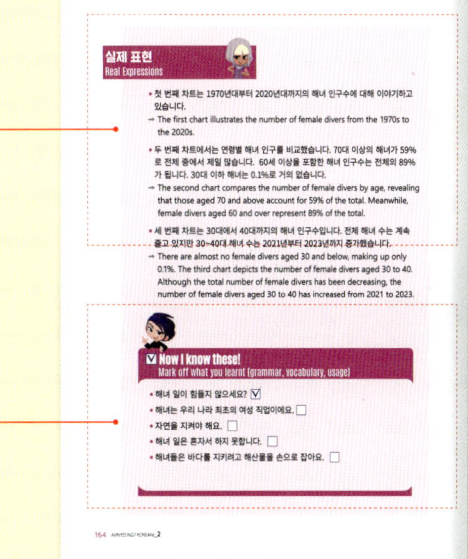

Unit structure 13

CHARACTERS

Sarang(사랑) Sarang has British-Korean background, and she is the manager of Sarang's guest house, located near Hongdae station. She also works part-time at a convenience store.

Haru(하루) Haru is a Japanese student interested in Korean dramas and K-pop. He is in Seoul to learn Korean.

Priya(프리야) Priya is from Indonesia. In her country, she works in a company. She is in Korea because she is interested in Korean culture.

Tao(타오) Tao is from China. He likes Korean food and he is into e-sports.

Caroline(캐롤라인) Caroline is from the US. She is professor of history at University, and she is in Korea to learn more about Korean culture and history.

Van Binh(반 빈) Van Binh is an IT expert from Vietnam visiting Korea to collaborate with a tech company. He looks forward to exploring new opportunities and building partnerships.

Maduka(마두카) Maduka is a university student from Nigeria. Is is traveling to Korea for pleasure.

Sophia(소피아)

Sophia is from France. She is passionate about sport, and she likes go hiking on Korean mountains.

Seon Deok(선덕) Seon Deok, a 70-year-old haenyeo from Jeju Island, has dedicated over 50 years to diving for seafood to support her family. And she is Sarang's grandmother.

Sam(샘)

Sam is from Australia. He loves cooking and loves Australian football and baseball.

Gabriel(가브리엘) Gabriel is from Canada. He studies architecture, and he is interested in Korean traditional houses. His grand-father participated in the Korean War.

Umid(우미드)

Umid is from Uzbekistan and has Korean ancestry. He is a professional graphic designer.

Jina Ssaem(지나쌤) Jina Ssaem is a Korean teacher in Annyeong? Korean! Series

Fatima (파티마)

Fatima, a teenager from Bolivia, is Gabriel's cousin and a big fan of K-fashion. She aspires to study in the biomedical field, following her mother's footsteps, as her mother works at a hospital in Bolivia called Corea.

왕이로소이다!

Sophia suggests wearing a hanbok to gain free entry into Gyeongbok Palace. They take beautiful photos and enjoy the feeling of having stepped back in time, experiencing a day as king and queen!

LEARNING OBJECTIVES

- Express future plans and activities
- Express possibilities and abilities
- Use vocabulary for clothes and dressing
- Recognise the main characteristics of Korean traditional dresses

GRAMMAR FOCUS

- -(으)ㄹ 거예요
- -(으)ㄹ 수 있다/없다

KEY GRAMMAR AND EXPRESSIONS

1. -(으)ㄹ 거예요

• **MEANING AND USAGE**

-(으)ㄹ 거예요 is attached to the base of processive and descriptive verbs. It indicates the future tense at an informal but polite level. In particular, it shows that something will probably happen in the future, and it is used to make a conjecture based on an objective ground.

• **STRUCTURE**

-을 거예요 is attached to verb bases ending with a consonant, while -ㄹ 거예요 is attached to verb bases ending with a vowel.

먹다 ➡ 먹 + 을 거예요 ➡ 먹을 거예요
가다 ➡ 가 + ㄹ 거예요 ➡ 갈 거예요
관광하다 ➡ 관광하 + ㄹ 거예요 ➡ 관광할 거예요

• **EXAMPLES**

샘: 사랑 씨, 다음 주말에 뭐 할 거예요?
Sarang, what are you going to do next weekend?

사랑: 소피아 씨하고 경복궁에 갈 거예요. 거기서 한복도 빌릴 거예요. 그 다음에 유튜브 비디오도 찍을 거예요.
I'm going to go to Gyeongbokgung Palace with Sophia We're going to rent a hanbok there. Then we're going to take a YouTube video.

소피아: 큰일났어요. 약속 시간이 얼마 남지 않았어요.
Oh no! We don't have much time left.

타오: 지하철을 탈까요? 그럼 늦지 않을 거예요. 그런데 사람이 많을 거예요.
Shall we take the subway? Then we won't be late. But it will be crowded.

2. -(으)ㄹ 수 있다/없다

• **MEANING AND USAGE**

-(으)ㄹ수 있다/없다 is attached to the base of action verbs to indicate whether something can or cannot be done. It can be used to express either the ability to do something, or the possibility to do something. When attached to descriptive verbs, it is used to make a conjecture about the possibility of being in a certain state.

• **STRUCTURE**

-을 수 있다/없다 is attached to verb bases ending with a consonant, while -ㄹ 수 있다/없다 is attached to verb bases ending with a vowel.

타다 ➡ 타 + ㄹ 수 있어요 ➡ 탈 수 있어요
찍다 ➡ 찍 + 을 수 있어요 ➡ 찍을 수 있어요
말하다 ➡ 말하 + ㄹ 수 없어요 ➡ 말할 수 없어요

• **EXAMPLES**

마두카
사랑 씨는 몇 개 언어 (말)할 수 있어요?
How many languages can you speak?

사랑
저는 한국어하고 영어 할 수 있어요. 그리고 스페인어도 조금 할 수 있어요.
I can speak Korean and English. I can also speak a little Spanish.

우미드
어디에서 한복을 빌릴 수 있어요?
Where can I borrow a Hanbok?

소피아
경복궁역 근처에서 빌릴 수 있어요!
You can borrow a Hanbok near Gyeongbokgung Station.

샘
사랑 씨, "파일을 찾을 수 없습니다." 이게 무슨 뜻이에요?
What does 'Can't find the file' mean?

사랑
아, 그건 "File Not Found"란 뜻이에요.
Oh, it means 'File Not Found.'

샘
그래요? 고마워요.
Really? Thank you.

 대화 DIALOGUE

Sarang, Sophia and Sam went to Gyeongbok Palace and visited the Hanbok rental house.

(Photo source: Nicola Fraschini)

 사랑: 와, 한복이 많네요!

 소피아: 사랑 씨, 우리 먼저 가방을 맡길까요?

 사랑: 네, 좋아요! 그런데 어디에 가방을 맡길 수 있어요?

 소피아: 지하 보관함에 맡길 수 있어요!

샘: 소피아 씨, 어떻게 이렇게 잘 알아요?

 소피아: 아, 구글에서 한복 렌탈을 검색했어요. 거기 리뷰에서 봤어요.

UNIT 1_ 왕이로소이다! 21

DIALOGUE

🗨 Roleplay the dialogue by substituting the colour-coded words or phrases with the prompts below.

가방을 맡기다 — 지하 보관함

옷을 입어 보다 — 저기 탈의실

사진/영상을 찍다 — 2층 포토존

읽기 READING

Pre-reading Activity

Link the pictures of the items on the left with the verb you use to indicate wearing them. Then, complete the sentences below with the most appropriate verb.

1. 소피아는 저고리와 바지를 _____. 그래서 무료로 경복궁에 들어갈 수 있어요.

2. 샘 씨는 갓을 _____. 정말 양반 같아요.

3. 마두카 씨는 두루마기만 _____. 그래서 무료로 경복궁에 들어갈 수 없어요.

4. 사랑 씨는 꽃신이 마음에 들어요. 그래서 내일 경복궁에서 꽃신을 _____.

READING

 **Reading Activity**

Sarang, Sam, and Sophia are planning their visit to the Royal Palace. Find out how much a regular ticket is, and what they need to wear to get free entry.

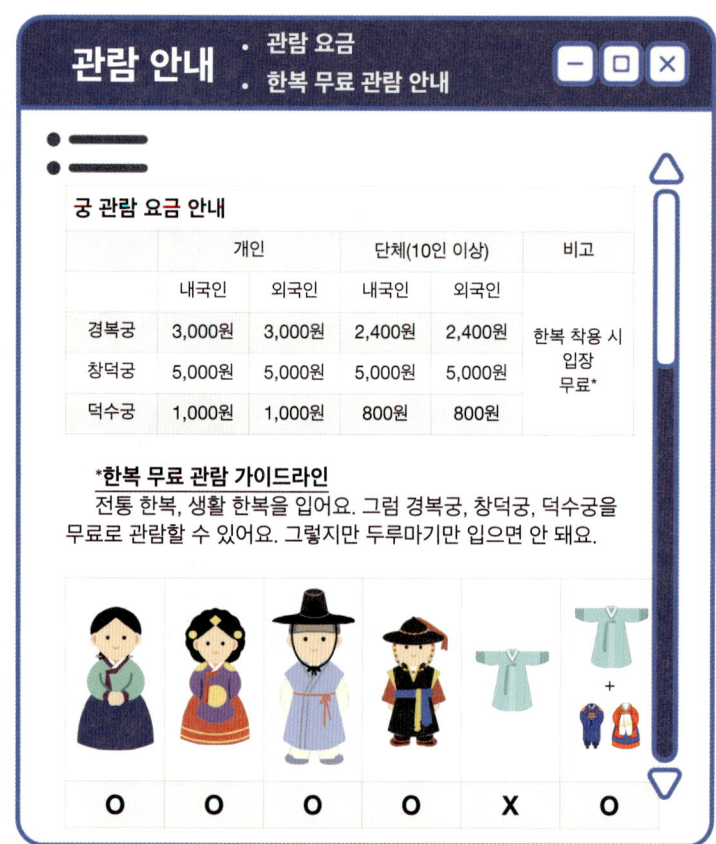

A. Tick off the statement if it is correct.

1. 경복궁 관람 요금은 내국인과 외국인이 달라요.

2. 한복을 안 입으면 창덕궁 관람 요금이 제일 비싸요.

3. 사랑 씨, 샘 씨와 소피아 씨는 한복을 입을 거예요. 그리고 경복궁과 덕수궁에 갈 거예요. 그래서 돈을 안 내요.

4. 소피아 씨는 치마와 저고리를 입었어요. 그리고 경복궁에 갈 거예요. 그래서 관람 요금은 3,000원이에요.

5. 샘 씨는 두루마기만 입었어요. 그래서 덕수궁을 무료로 구경할 수 있어요.

READING

공지 사항

경복궁 프랑스어 안내 서비스!

우리 궁궐에 한국어, 영어, 일본어, 중국어 4개 언어 안내 서비스가 있습니다. 다음 달부터 프랑스어 안내 서비스도 시작합니다.
운영 시간은 수요일/목요일 오전 11시와 오후 3시입니다.

☎ 문의 02-3700-3900

오늘 하루 그만 보기	닫기

B. Answer to the following questions.

1. 이번 공지 사항 내용이 뭐예요?

2. 지금 경복궁에서 어떤 안내 언어 서비스를 받을 수 있어요?

3. 다음 달부터 어떤 언어 안내 서비스를 시작할 거예요?

4. 프랑스어 안내 서비스는 언제 받을 수 있어요?

After-reading Activity

Look at the notes in Sophia's diary, and describe what she will be doing next weekend.

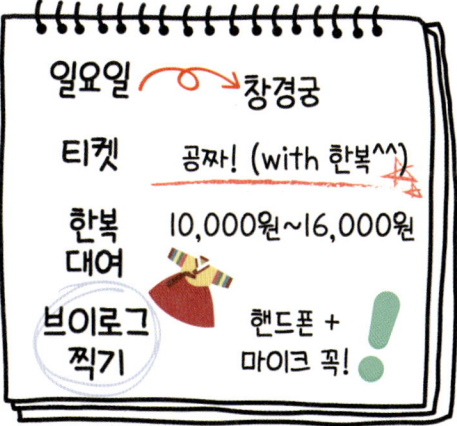

일요일 → 창경궁
티켓   공짜! (with 한복^^)
한복 대여   10,000원~16,000원
브이로그 찍기   핸드폰 + 마이크 꼭!

_____
_____
_____
_____

듣기 LISTENING

 **Pre-listening Activity**

Match the colours to the correct words/expressions.

| 파란색 | 하얀색 | 노란색 | 주황색 | 빨간색 | 초록색 | 남색 |

🎧 Look at the colours of the clothing in each picture and fill in the gaps using the appropriate words from the list below.

칠했어요, 하얀색, 썼어요, 신었어요, 보라색, 노란색, 입었어요, 파란색, 치마

E.g., 건물에 여러 가지 색깔을 <u>칠했어요.</u>

①    ②    ③    ④

1. 저 옷에 _____와/과 빨간색과 노란색과 _____이/가 있어요.

2. 저 옷은 빨간색이에요. 왕이 _____.

3. 저고리는 _____이에요. _____은/는 초록색이에요. 신발은 _____이에요.

4. 저 사람은 검은색 갓을 _____. 그리고 자주색 신발을 _____.

LISTENING

 **Listening Activity**

Sophia is podcasting on YouTube about her plans to visit Gyeongbok Palace next weekend. What did she say she will do next weekend?

A. Listen to the audio and then select any correct statement.

1. 소피아 씨는 프랑스어로 경복궁 안내를 받을 거예요. ☐
2. 소피아 씨는 저고리만 파란색으로 입을 거예요. ☐
3. 한복 가게에서 한복 머리 스타일링을 받을 수 없어요. ☐
4. 경복궁에서 건축 사진을 찍을 거예요. ☐
5. 경복궁 동영상은 두 달 뒤에 업로드될 거예요. ☐

B. List two reasons why she wants to visit the Hanbok rental shop early.

소피아 씨는 왜 한복 가게에 일찍 갈 거예요? 이유 두 가지를 쓰세요.

1. _____.
2. _____.

1 Describe the image and explain to your partner what they can and cannot do in Gyeongbok Palace and its surroundings. Then, create your mini-dialogue using -(으)ㄹ 수 있다/없다 and -(으)ㄹ 거예요.

✅ 할 수 있어요.	🚫 할 수 없어요.
e.g. 한복을 입어요. 그럼 경복궁에 무료로 들어갈 수 있어요.	

ACTIVITY

2 What would you like to do if you go to Gyeongbok Palace? Are you planning to borrow a hanbok there? What colours do you want to wear?

3 **Translation Challenge**: Look up the meaning of Gyeongbok Palace in the dictionary. Then, interpret the palace's name in your own words in English, for example, by giving it a nickname that reflects the Gyeongbok Palace's (경복궁) meaning.

"왕이로소이다!"

Hanbok in the K-Wave Era

The hanbok, Korea's traditional clothing, has recently attracted more attention due to the expanding K-wave. Ranging from classic hanboks seen at temples and traditional restaurants to casual versions for everyday use, this iconic attire elegantly fuses heritage with modernity. Younger generations, especially Millennials and Gen Z, are adopting the "fashion hanbok," which incorporates contemporary styles with classic silhouettes. These refreshed designs make the hanbok more suitable for daily wear while respecting cultural traditions. In various locations, wearing a hanbok can even provide free access to cultural sites, enhancing its growing allure.

The title of this unit, (왕이로소이다), alludes to a 1923 poem by Sayong Hong and a 2012 Korean film, suggesting that nowadays, individuals can assume the role of a king simply by wearing royal attire.

(Video Source: Visit Korean Heritage Campaign)

K-MEDIA CORNER

Wearing hanbok, Korea's traditional attire, especially at historical sites like a Gyeongbok Palace, has become a cherished cultural experience. This practice is often featured in K-dramas. **Love in the Moonlight** (2016) showcases the beauty of the hanbok within the Joseon dynasty, inspiring viewers to partake in hanbok experiences at palaces.

Recent K-dramas elegantly highlight Korea's palaces and hanbok (한복), immersing viewers in traditional culture. **The Red Sleeve** (옷소매 붉은 끝동) explores the romance and intricate dynamics of court life, featuring characters in exquisite hanboks (한복) that signify their status. Additionally, a modernised version of the hanbok suitable for everyday wear appears in *Jeongnyeon: The Star is Born* (정년이), both in the drama and the webtoon.

 What attracts Generation Z or young people to wear hanboks?

 Should the hanbok be preserved in its traditional form without any modern modifications?

 Do you believe allowing free entries at historical sites for wearing a traditional dress is an effective way to maintain tradition, and why?

[이미지 출처: 네이버/유튜브]

실제 표현
Real Expressions

- 경복궁 프랑스어 정규 안내 해설을 다음과 같이 운영하여 관람객 서비스 향상에 최선을 다하고자 합니다.
→ We aim to enhance our service to visitors by conducting the regular French guided tour of Gyeongbok Palace as follows.

- 청바지에 저고리만 착용하거나, 한복 하의에 티셔츠를 입은 경우는 무료 관람이 불가능합니다.
→ Visitors dressed solely in a jeogori (traditional Korean jacket) paired with jeans or a T-shirt combined with hanbok bottoms will not be granted free admission.

- 머리손질, 댕기, 헤어밴드, 속치마, 손가방, 사물함 모두 무료로 제공해 드립니다.
→ Hair styling, braided hair with a ribbon, hairbands, underskirts, handbags, and lockers are available at no additional cost.

☑ Now I know these!
Mark off what you learnt (grammar, vocabulary, usage)

- 관람 요금 안내 ☑
- 어디에서 옷을 입어 볼 수 있어요? ☐
- 저고리와 바지 ☐
- 외국인, 내국인 ☐
- 착용하다 ☐
- 입장 ☐
- 한복 렌탈 샵에서 한복 머리 스타일링을 받을 거예요. ☐

02과

내가 니 친구야?

Umid, an employee at K-Company, faces challenges in effectively using language in various contexts, leading to confusion about when and how to communicate with others. He shares his experiences to shed light on these difficulties.

LEARNING OBJECTIVES

- Make comparisons
- Use language in informal social exchanges
- Understand the difference between formal and informal contexts
- Use vocabulary related to roles in professional/working life
- Understand the structure of a Korean working environment

GRAMMAR FOCUS

- 반말
- 보다
- 제일

KEY GRAMMAR AND EXPRESSIONS

1. 반말

• MEANING AND USAGE

반말 is a speech level used between intimate people, i.e. close to each other, and people of the same age, and for this reason it is often called intimate speech level. It is used, for example, among classmates (same age) and close friends. When people first meet, they may want to use the informal polite speech, and then they may switch to the intimate level once they become more intimate. In the case of two intimate people of different ages, generally the older person uses the intimate speech level, and the younger person the informal polite level (see vol. 1). Using the intimate level outside of these specific contexts is rude and impolite. In the workplace, individuals typically use polite language, but they may resort to informal speech in private conversations if they are sufficiently close to one another.

• STRUCTURE

In comparison to the informal polite speech level, when using 반말, most changes occur in verb endings and pronouns. The most notable characteristic is that 요 is dropped from verbal endings. See Appendix 2 (p.168) for complete details.

저는 술을 못 마셔요. ➡ 나는 술 못 마셔.
저희 반말을 할까요? ➡ 우리 반말을 할까?
소피아 씨는 파란색 한복을 빌릴 거예요. ➡ 소피아는 파란색 한복을 빌릴거야.

• EXAMPLES

하루: 마두카 씨 몇 살이에요?
Maduka, how old are you?

마두카: 저는 스물 두 살이에요. 하루 씨는요?
I am 22 years old, what about you?

하루: 저도요! 그럼 마두카 씨, 우리 반말해요. 어때요?
Me too! Then, Maduka, let's use informal language. How about that?

마두카: 네. 좋아요! 아니, 응. 좋아. 그렇게 하자!
Yes, let's do it! No, yes. Alright, let's do it!

사랑이 엄마: 사랑아, 밥 먹어. Sarang, eat your dinner.

사랑: 네, 알겠어요.. Yes, I will.

2. 보다

• **MEANING AND USAGE**

보다 is a particle used for comparisons, like "than" in English, indicating that something is more (or less) than something else. 더 means "more", and 덜 means "less." These words are often used with 보다, such as in the phrases 보다 더 or 보다 덜.

• **STRUCTURE**

보다 is attached to nouns ending in either vowels or consonants. 보다 is attached to the noun that becomes the reference for the comparison.

E.g. Subject 이/가 or 은/는 + **Noun보다** (더/덜) + verbs.

Subject → Element of direct comparison
Noun → Reference

• **EXAMPLES**

마두카: 타오 씨와 우미드 씨 중에 누가 나이가 (더) 많아요? Who is older, Tao or Umid?

타오: 우미드 씨가 저보다 더 나이가 많아요. 그래서 우미드 씨가 형이에요. Umid is older than me, I call him 'hyeong'—that's just what we say for older guys in Korean.

캐롤라인: 사랑 씨, 저는 주말에 강릉에 가고 싶어요. 교통편 좀 추천해 주세요. Sarang, I want to go to Gangneung on the weekend. Please recommend some transportation options.

사랑: 버스가 편해요. 그런데 주말에는 차가 많이 막혀요. 그래서 KTX를 타세요. KTX가 버스보다 빨라요. Buses are convenient; however, there are many traffic jams on weekends. Therefore, take the KTX. It is faster than the bus.

3. 제일

• **MEANING AND USAGE**

제일 is an adverb used to indicate that, among a group or a category, something is "the most".

• **STRUCTURE**

제일 is generally used in front of processive and descriptive verbs.

E.g. Subject 이/가 or 은/는 + **제일** + verbs.

• **EXAMPLES**

한반도에서 백두산이 제일 높은 산이에요.
➞ Mt. Baekdu is the highest mountain in the Korean peninsula.

우미드 씨는 빨간색을 제일 좋아해요.
➞ Umid likes the colour red the most.

회사 생활에서 뭐가 제일 중요해요?
➞ What's the most important aspect of work life?

샘

안녕하세요? 이거 호주로 보내고 싶어요. 어떤 게 제일 빨라요?
Hello! I'd like to send this to Australia. What's the quickest option?

우체국 직원

아, 네. 국제특급이 제일 빨리 갈 거예요.
Yes, international express will be the fastest.

샘

그럼 국제특급으로 보내 주세요.
Please send it via international express.

대화 DIALOGUE

Umid is feeling down about the company's project results, and his close colleague is checking in to see what happened.

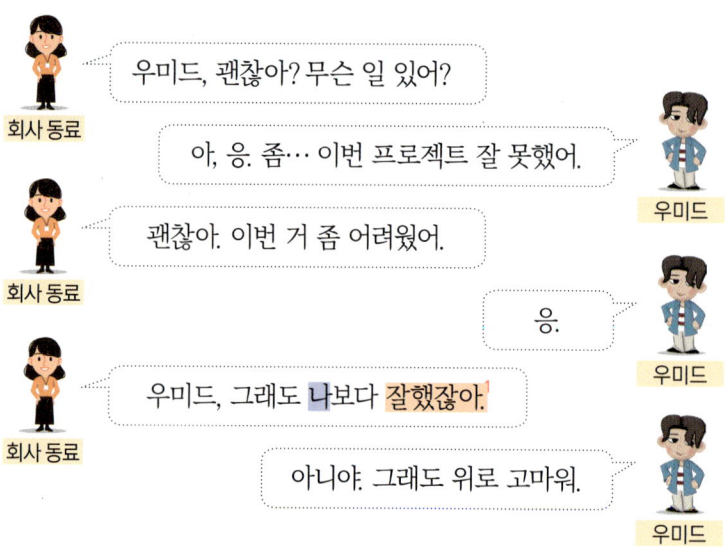

회사 동료: 우미드, 괜찮아? 무슨 일 있어?
우미드: 아, 응. 좀… 이번 프로젝트 잘 못했어.
회사 동료: 괜찮아. 이번 거 좀 어려웠어.
우미드: 응.
회사 동료: 우미드, 그래도 **나**보다 **잘했잖아**.[1]
우미드: 아니야. 그래도 위로 고마워.

🗨️ **Roleplay the dialogue by substituting the colour-coded words or phrases with the prompts below.**

나	잘했잖아
다른 신입 사원	열심히 했잖아
누구	많이 일했잖아

---

[1] The verb ending -잖아 in this context means "as you know," stressing that the listener already knows or is aware of what is said.

읽기 READING

Pre-reading Activity

Umid is now working as a designer in a company. He saw this flyer on the notice board, but he could not fully understand it. Help Umid understand the meaning of the words circled in red! What is the flyer about?

📖 **Pair the word with its closest meaning in the box.**

회식, 참석, 자세하다, 환영하다, 신입 사원

_____	저는 며칠 전에 이 회사에 취직했어요.
회식	회사 사람들하고 저녁에 다 같이 식사해요. 그리고 가끔 같이 노래방에도 가요.
_____	여러분이 회사에 처음 왔어요. 그럼 회사 사람들이 축하해 줘요.
_____	A부터 Z까지 알 수 있어요.
_____	모임이 있어요. 그럼 거기에 가요.

READING

Reading Activity

After getting the email about the function, Umid messaged his older co-worker, Jisoo. Read their chat and answer the following questions: What is Umid worried about? Why does Jisoo address Umid with intimate language in their texts?

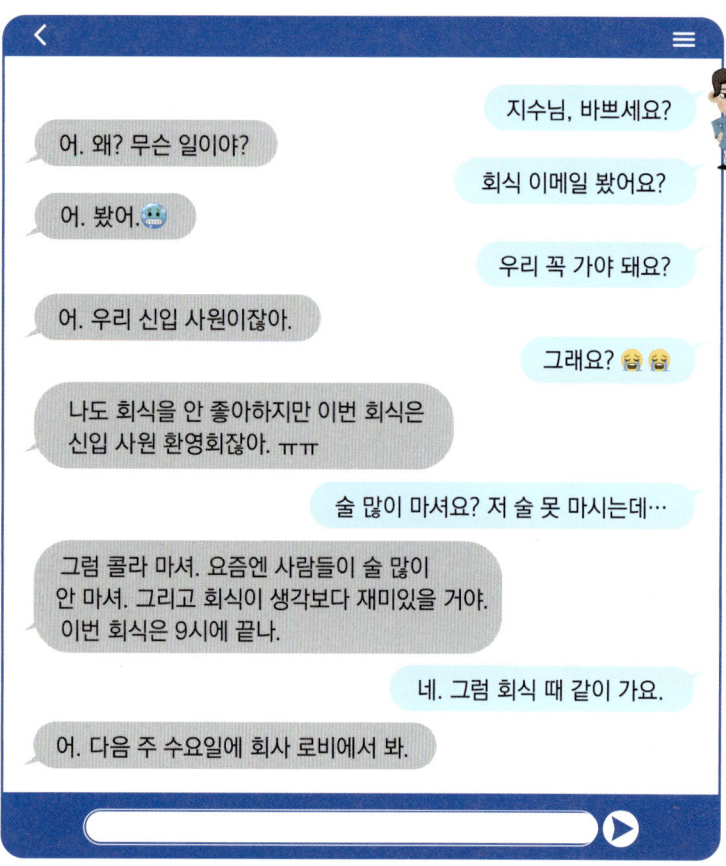

A. Answer the following questions using information from the reading text. Circle the sections of the text that contain the answers.

1. 우미드 씨는 누구한테 이 메세지를 보냈어요?
2. 지수 씨는 왜 회식에 갈 거예요?
3. 우미드 씨는 왜 회식에 안 가고 싶어해요?
4. 요즘 회식은 어때요?
5. 회사 사람은 회식에 대해 어떻게 생각해요?
6. 이번 회식은 몇 시에 끝나요?

READING

B. Answer to the following questions.

1. 회식이 뭐예요?
2. 여러분은 회식에 가고 싶어요? 안 가고 싶어요? 왜요?
3. 한국 회식 문화에 대해 어떤 것을 알아요? 어디에서 들었어요?
4. 한국 회식 문화에 대해 어떻게 생각하세요? 여러분 나라의 회식은 어때요?

 After-reading Activity

Umid must inform the assistant manager (김 대리님) by this Friday about his attendance at the work function (회식). Please write an email to the assistant manager on behalf of Umid, including a suitable subject line.

보낸 사람: umid.uz@seouldesign.co.kr

받는 사람: dongsik.kim@seouldesign.co.kr

Re:

김 대리님께,

안녕하세요?

....

....

....

안녕히 계세요.

우미드 올림

 **Pre-listening Activity**

Find the meanings of the expressions in the boxes and use them to fill in the blanks. Then write a mini-dialogue using some of them.

```
        말실수              이렇게 말했어요.
존댓말
        반말                이해해 줘요
```

1. 할머니한테 ___존댓말___ 을/를 써요.

2. 엄마가 아이한테 _____ 을/를 써요.

3. 제 친구는 부모님보다 저를 더 잘 _____.

4. (저는) 어제 회사에서 사장님께 _____ 을/를 했어요.
   사장님은 저한테 "우미드 씨, 식사 잘 했어요?"라고 말했어요.
   그런데 저는 "네. 사장님은?" _____.

_____
_____
_____
_____
_____
_____
_____

LISTENING

 **Listening Activity**

Sarang and Umid are discussing their experiences with using 반말 and 존댓말. What common mistakes did they make?

A. Listen to the audio and then select any correct statement.

1. 우미드 씨는 지난주보다 이번 주에 더 바빠요. ☐
2. 우미드 씨 회사 사람들은 다 친절해요. ☐
3. 우미드 씨 회사의 대리님은 다른 사람보다 조금 더 친절해요. ☐
4. 우미드 씨와 사랑 씨는 아직도 존댓말과 반말이 제일 어려워요. ☐
5. 우미드 씨와 사랑 씨는 말실수를 자주 안 해요. ☐

B. Ask and answer the following questions with your partners.

1. 우미드 씨는 왜 "대리님이 제일 친절하세요"라고 말했어요?
2. 우미드 씨는 점심 때 대리님한테 무슨 말실수를 했어요?
3. 우미드 씨와 사랑 씨는 한국말 중에서 뭐가 제일 어려워요?
4. 사랑 씨는 왜 할머니를 제일 좋아해요?
5. 마지막에 우미드 씨는 왜 웃었어요?

C. What could Sarang say to her grandmother this time, correcting her previous mistake? Finish the sentence accordingly.

사랑: 할머니 잘 _____.

활동 ACTIVITY

1 Have you ever made a similar mistake while speaking another language, like Umid or Sarang? Share your experience with your partner, and then discuss the main reasons behind that mistake. Is it due to cultural differences, the language itself, or something else?

■ 무슨 말했어요?

■ 누구한테 그 말을 했어요?

■ 그 다음에 어떻게 됐어요?

■ 그래서 그 말은 원래 어떻게 말해야 돼요?

ACTIVITY

2 Does your language have 반말 or 존댓말? If so, what are the similarities and differences? If not, how would you explain these concepts to someone unfamiliar with them?

_____
_____
_____
_____

3 **Translation Challenge:** Read the main listening script, then translate the conversation into English as naturally and accurately as possible. You can also compare your translation with a machine translator to see the differences.

"K-문화: "내가 니 친구야?"

반말 VS. 존댓말
Politeness in the Korean Language

The Korean language intricately incorporates hierarchy and politeness into everyday communication through 존댓말 (formal speech) and 반말 (informal speech). While 존댓말 is essential for showing respect, using it in the wrong context can come across as distant or overly formal.

On the other hand, speaking in 반말 with someone older or in a higher position is often viewed as disrespectful. Such mistakes frequently lead to humorous yet awkward moments, especially for language learners. Mastering when and how to use these speech levels is key to navigating relationships in Korean society. Though it's never easy, some believe that these distinctions may gradually loosen over time as society evolves, with fewer extended family ties and declining birth rates potentially playing a role.

Extra reading:
- BBC "Where asking someone's age isn't rude", 3 January 2022
  https://www.bbc.com/travel/article/20211214-where-asking-someonesage-isnt-rude Accessed 12th April 2025
- McKinsey & Company, "The power of language: Navigating global legal practice"
  https://www.mckinsey.com/featured-insights/in-the-balance/the-power-of-language-navigating-global-legal-practice Accessed 12th April 2025

K-MEDIA CORNER

Korean dramas often explore the complexities of language and relationships, particularly through the use of honorifics and informal speech (반말). In *Incomplete Life* (미생), you can learn which languages levels are appropriate for the various workplace positions. In *Reply 1988* (응답하라 1988), characters navigate family and friendship dynamics, often switching between formal and informal speech to reflect their closeness. *Fight for My Way* (쌈 마이웨이) humorously portrays the struggle between friends and couples as they decide when it's appropriate to drop honorifics and use banmal. Because *This Is My First Life* (이번 생은 처음이라) shows how the use of language changes as characters grow closer, emphasizing the impact of speech on relationships. These dramas highlight how Korean titles and language reflect respect, familiarity, and the nuances of social hierarchy, creating both humorous and heartwarming moments.

 How do K-dramas use the transition from formal speech to 반말 to show changes in relationships between characters?

 What does the use of language in these dramas teach us about respect and social norms in Korean culture?

[이미지 출처: 네이버/유튜브]

실제 표현
Real Expressions

- 이번 프로젝트 잘 못한 것 같아.
→ I feel I didn't perform well on this project.

- 우리 팀에서 누구보다 많이 일했잖아.
→ You contributed more than anyone else on our team.

- 그래도 위로해 줘서 고마워.
→ Even so, I appreciate your encouragement.

- 회식 참석 여부를 이번 주 금요일까지 메일로 보내 주세요.
→ Could you please email me by this Friday to confirm your attendance at the work function dinner?

- 나도 회식을 안 좋아하긴 하지만 이번 회식은 신입 사원 환영회니까 가야 할 것 같아.
→ I'm not particularly fond of work function dinners either, but since this is a welcome party for new employees, I believe I should attend

☑ Now I know these!
Mark off what you learnt (grammar, vocabulary, usage)

- 나보다 열심히 했잖아! ☑
- 위로 ☐
- 신입 사원 ☐
- 참석할 수 있어요. ☐
- 회식 ☐
- 존댓말, 반말 ☐
- 말실수 ☐

03과

국가대표

In a thrilling adventure, Sam and Priya are joined by their ski enthusiast friend from Australia as they travel to Korea, visiting the iconic ski resort of the 2018 Winter Olympics. They dive into Korean winter sports culture, explore local attractions, and learn essential expressions for making recommendations.

LEARNING OBJECTIVES

- Express necessity
- Understand short safety instructions and local geography
- Use vocabulary to plan for leisure activities

GRAMMAR FOCUS

- -아/어야 하다
- -고
- 하고

KEY GRAMMAR AND EXPRESSIONS

1. -아/어야 하다

• MEANING AND USAGE

-아/어야 하다 is attached to the base of action verbs to indicate something that has to be done, needs to be done, or must be done. The 하다 part can be replaced by 되다, as both take on the exact same meaning in this grammar structure, resulting in the form -아/어야 되다 as -아/어야 하다.

• STRUCTURE

-아야 하다 is attached to verb bases containing ㅏ or ㅗ, while -어야 하다 is attached to verb bases containing other vowels. 하다 becomes 해야 해요. -아/어야 되다 is also used with the same meaning and in the same contexts.

타다 ➡ 타 + 아야 해요 ➡ 타야 해요
입다 ➡ 입 + 어야 해요 ➡ 입어야 해요
준비하다 ➡ 준비하 + 여야 해요 ➡ 준비해야 해요

• EXAMPLES

샘: 스키를 탈 거예요?
Are you going skiing?

프리야: 네. 스키를 탈 거예요. 그런데 스키 장비와 옷을 빌려야 해요. 어디에서 빌릴 수 있어요?
Yes, I'm going skiing. But I need to rent ski equipment and clothes. Where can I rent them?

샘: 스키장 렌탈샵에서 빌릴 수 있는데 신분증이 있어야 해요.
You can rent them at the ski resort rental shop, but you need to have your ID with you.

프리야: 스키 장갑도 빌릴 수 있어요?
Can I rent ski gloves as well?

샘: 아니요. 스키 장갑은 사야 돼요.
No, you have to buy them.

손님: 저는 스키장에 가야 해요. 저기서 셔틀버스를 타요?
I need to go to the ski resort. Can I take the shuttle bus from there?

안내 직원: 네. 그런데 지금 시간에는 셔틀버스가 없어요. 그래서 스키장까지 택시를 타야 돼요.
Yes; however, there are currently no shuttle buses available at this time. Therefore, you will need to take a taxi to the ski resort.

2. -고

타오: 저는 울릉도에 가요. 어느 배를 타야 돼요?
I'm going to Ulleungdo. Which ferry should I take?

항구 직원: 저기 빨간색 배를 타세요.
Take the red ferry over there.

• MEANING AND USAGE

-고 is attached to the base of action and descriptive verbs to connect two or more actions or states. Depending on the context, it can indicate that the two actions happen together at the same time (first example below), or one after the other (first dialogue below).

• STRUCTURE

-고 is attached to all verb bases, both consonant-ending and vowel-ending.

사다 ➡ 사 + 고 ➡ 사고
보내다 ➡ 보내 + 고 ➡ 보내고
하다 ➡ 하 + 고 ➡ 하고

• EXAMPLES

이 스키장은 서울에서 가깝고 저렴해요. 그리고 평일에는 사람들이 별로 없고 좋아요.
➡ This ski resort is near Seoul and is affordable. Additionally, there aren't many visitors on weekdays, which is nice.

캐롤라인: 지금 이렇게 음식을 주문하고 이따가 더 시킬까요?
Should we order food now and order more later?

타오: 네! 좋아요!
Yes, that's fine!

반빈: 우리 영화 보고 밥 먹을까? 밥 먹고 영화 볼까?
Should we watch a movie and then eat, or eat and then watch a movie?

반빈 친구: 밥 먹고 영화 보자. 아직 시간 있어.
Let's eat, and then watch a movie. We still have time.

3. 하고

• **MEANING AND USAGE**

하고 is a particle used to connect two nouns. It means "and".

• **STRUCTURE**

하고 is attached to both nouns ending with vowels and nouns ending with consonants.

Noun with vowel ending: 잡채하고 김치전
Noun with consonant ending: 여권하고 비자

• **EXAMPLES**

캐롤라인: 한국 야구하고 미국 야구 중에서 뭐가 더 재밌어요?
Which is more fun, Korean baseball or American baseball?

샘: 저는 둘 다 재미있어요!
I enjoy both!

손님: 여기요! 닭강정하고 참치 김밥 하나 주세요.
Excuse me! I'd like some Korean sweet glazed fried chicken and one tuna gimbap, please.

사장님: 네. 조금만 기다려 주세요.
Sure. Just a moment, please.

반 빈: 저하고 제 친구는 베트남 사람이에요.
My friend and I are from Vietnam.

사랑: 만나서 반갑습니다.
Nice to meet you.

대화 DIALOGUE

Sam is planning to visit a ski resort in Korea with his Australian friend so he is seeking advice from Priya, who visited a ski resort with her family last year.

 샘: 프리야 씨, 다음 달에 제 친구가 호주에서 와요.

 프리야: 와~ 뭐 할 거예요?

 샘: 제 친구가 스키를 좋아해요. 그래서 같이 스키장에 갈 거예요. 뭘 준비해야 해요?

 프리야: 리프트권을 미리 사야 돼요.

 샘: 아 그래요?

 프리야: 네. 그런데 스키하고 스키복은 쉽게 빌릴 수 있어요.

 샘: 알려 줘서 고마워요. 프리야 씨.

Roleplay the dialogue by substituting the colour-coded words or phrases with the prompts below.

- 리프트권을 (미리) 사다
- KTX 기차표를 예약하다
- 셔틀버스 시간을 (미리) 알다
- 스키 장갑하고 고글을 사다

읽기 READING

Pre-reading Activity

Sam, his Australian friend and Priya are at a ski resort in Gangwon-do (강원도). They review the safety instructions before renting their gear and selecting the slopes. Sam explains some of the words to his friends. He helps clarify these terms by using simpler expressions. Match the words on the left with the expressions on the right.

주의사항 — 모자를 써요. 신발을 신어요. 장갑을 껴요.

안전 — 갑자기 안 움직여요.

착용하다 — 어떤 것을 조심해야 해요.

선택하다 — 안 위험해요. 사고가 없어요.

멈추다 — 어떤 것을 골라야 해요.

READING

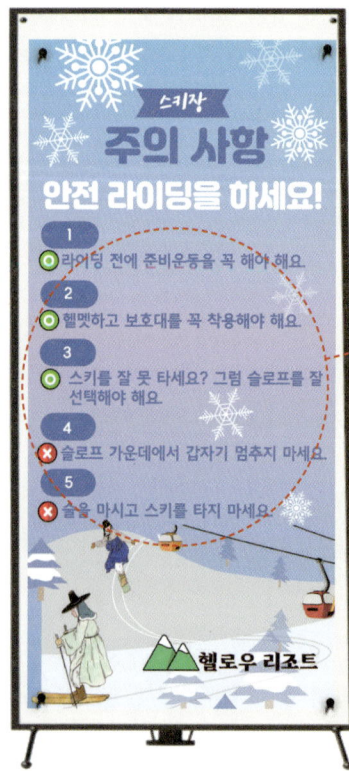

Reading Activity

Read the following safety guidelines for the ski slope. What must you do before starting to ski? What shouldn't you do?

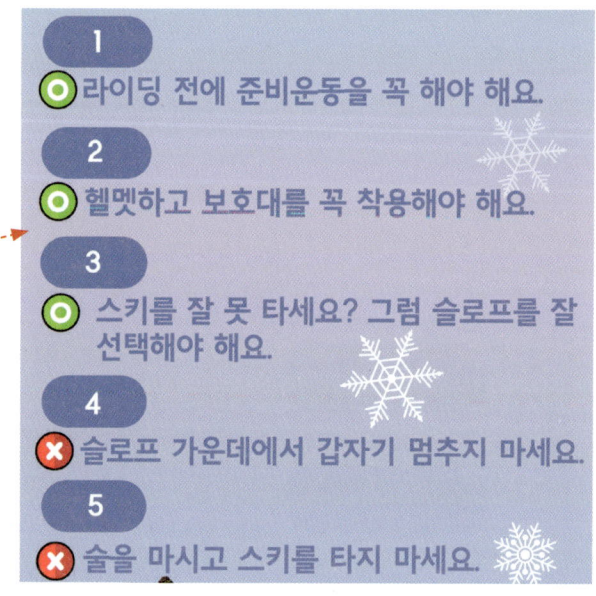

A. Check off the statement if it is correct.

1. 라이딩 후에 준비 운동을 해야 돼요.
2. 보통 사람들이 헬멧만 써야 해요.
3. 저는 스키를 잘 타요. 그래서 어려운 슬로프에서 스키를 탈 수 있어요.
4. 슬로프 가운데에서 갑자기 멈춰요. 그럼 안전해요.
5. 사람들이 술을 마셨어요. 그래서 스키를 못 타요.

B. Answer to the following questions.

1. 라이딩 전에 뭐 해야 해요?
2. 스키를 타요. 그럼 무엇을 꼭 착용해야 해요? 왜요?
3. 여러분이 스키를 잘 못 타요. 그럼 어떤 슬로프를 선택해야 해요?
4. 여러분이 스키장에 친구들하고 갈 거예요. 그럼 어떤 것을 준비할 거예요?

READING

 **After-reading Activity**

Sam, his friend and Priya now need to rent their gear and buy the tickets.

1. First, check the vocabulary from the information table with your partners.

2. Then, role-play the conversation between Sam and his friends, and between Sam and the ticket seller.

시간대	오전	오후	야간	주간
이용 시간	9:00-12:00	13:00-17:00	18:30-21:30	9:00-17:00

구분	스키 렌탈	스키 부츠 렌탈	스키 옷 렌탈
오전, 오후, 야간	28,000원	10,000원	15,000원
주간	32,000원	15,000원	25,000원

E.g. **Role-play 1**

🧑 언제 스키를 탈까요?
🧑 오후에 타요. 근데 저는 스키가 없어요. 그래서 이따가 스키를 빌려야 해요.

E.g. **Role-play 2**

🧑 오후에 스키를 탈 거예요. 스키 렌탈이 얼마예요?
🧑 스키 렌탈은 28,000원이에요. 부츠는 10,000원이에요.
🧑 그럼 스키하고 부츠 둘 다 주세요.

 **Pre-listening Activity**

Listen to the audio files, complete the mini-dialogues by selecting the expressions you heard.

1. 어디에서 스키장 (**마을 버스를 타야 해요? / 셔틀버스를 타야 해요?**)

   역 밖으로 나가세요. 그 다음에 횡단보도를 건너세요. 그럼 축제 포스터가 보일 거에요. 그 앞에서 타세요.

   감사합니다.

2. 이 스키장은 (**뭐가 좋아요? / 뭐가 좋았어요?**)

   아. 이 스키장은 셔틀버스가 (**더 많고 사우나 시설이 좋아요. / 더 많고 숙박 시설이 좋아요.**) 그리고 더 싸요.

LISTENING

 **Listening Activity**

Sam, his friend, and Priya are arriving at Jinbu Station in Gangwon-do and now plan to take the resort shuttle bus to the Pyeongchang ski resort. Where should they go to catch the shuttle bus?

A. Listen to the audio and then select any correct statement.

1. 프리야와 샘은 셔틀버스 장소를 잘 몰라.　☐
2. 셔틀버스는 녹색 포스터 근처에서 타.　☐
3. 평창 스키장은 다른 스키장 보다 셔틀버스가 안 많아.　☐

B. Ask and answer the following questions with your partners.

1. 프리야는 지난번에 어떻게 평창 스키장에 왔어?
2. 샘하고 프리야는 처음에 셔틀버스 장소를 몰랐어. 그런데 어떻게 나중에 탈 수 있었어?
3. (네 생각에) 기차역 매점 아주머니는 셔틀버스 장소를 왜 잘 아셔?

C. 샘과 친구들은 왜 이 스키장을 골랐어?

_____
_____
_____
_____

활동 ACTIVITY

1 When people visit certain places that you know well, do you give them advice by suggesting they try specific foods or visit particular locations? In this context, you can also use the grammar -아/어야 하다 in everyday Korean language, which translates to terms like "must visit places or items" in English.

2 Here are some examples of activities, places, and food that people recommend when travelling in Gangwon-do. Use the information from the cue cards provided to offer advice!

프리야 씨,
저 다음 주에 강릉에
놀러 가요!

아, 그래요?
그럼 커피 거리는 꼭 가야 해요!
강릉역에서 가까워요.
카페에서 커피 마시고 케이크도
꼭 먹어야 돼요.

ACTIVITY

3 You can also introduce your local must-see places and mention what people should try there.

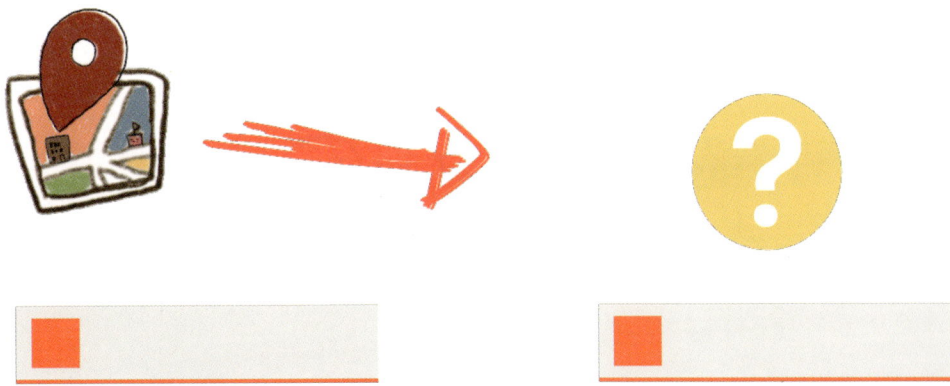

"국가대표"

Winter sports in Korea

Winter in Korea is brimming with outdoor fun, led by ice skating, skiing, and snowboarding at the centre of the country's cold-weather charm. Gangwon-do, known for its abundant snowfall, hosts popular ski resorts like Pyeongchang, which drew global attention during the 2018 Winter Olympics.

These resorts feature top-notch facilities, challenging slopes, and stunning snow-filled views, attracting both locals and visitors eager to embrace the season. In cities such as Seoul, ice rinks spring up in parks and plazas, turning them into festive hubs where families, friends, and couples share in the seasonal excitement.

K-MEDIA CORNER

In the film industry, sports themes serve as powerful storytelling tools. They present incredible challenges and show how people overcome them from various perspectives such as athletes, coaches, parents, agents, and amateur players. If we narrow it down to the Winter Olympics, there are all-time classic movies to enjoy during the season, such as **Cool Runnings** (1993) and **Eddie the Eagle** (2015). In Korea, one of the most well-known sports movies is **Take Of** (국가대표), which follows the true story of the Korea's Olympic ski jump team that participated in the 1998 Nagano Winter Olympics. The movie's original soundtrack, "Butterfly" from Loveholics (러브홀릭스), is also worth considering; the lyrics are very inspiring and uplifting!

 What role do sports play in people's lives? What kinds of extraordinary efforts and contributions do athletes make, as shown in *Take Off* or any other sports film you've seen?

 How do Korean sports movies compare to others in illustrating how Korean culture is represented in winter sports?

The movie OST
"Butterfly"

[이미지 출처: 네이버/유튜브]

실제 표현
Real Expressions

- 지하철을 기다릴 때 노란색 안전선 뒤에서 기다려야 합니다.
→ When waiting for the subway, please stay behind the yellow safety line.

- 장비 렌탈할 때 신분증을 지참해야 돼요.
→ You need to bring your ID for equipment rental.

- 바로 사용하기 편리하고 저렴합니다.
→ It's easy and affordable to use immediately.

- 실력에 맞는 코스를 선택해야 합니다.
→ Choose a course that aligns with your skill level.

- 거기 가세요? 그럼 ○○은 꼭 가셔야 해요. 그리고 ○○도 꼭 들러서 구경해 보셔야 해요!
→ Are you heading there? If so, you definitely should visit 00, and don't forget to check out ○○ while you're at it!

- 지금 안 가면 1년을 기다려야 해요!
→ If you don't go now, you'll have to wait an entire year!

☑ Now I know these!
Mark off what you learnt (grammar, vocabulary, usage)

- 리프트권을 미리 사야 해요. ☑
- 주의사항 ☐
- 선택하다 ☐
- 술을 마시고 스키를 타지 마세요. ☐
- 시간이 남다. ☐
- 숙박 시설도 넓고 깨끗해. ☐
- 커피 거리하고 울릉도는 꼭 가야 돼. ☐

04과

보물 1호, 응원봉

Haru takes her mother to a K-pop concert, where Haru cheers with her no.1 most treasured item, the light stick. The energy is electric, and even the non-fans can't help but join the fun. It's a night filled with music, dancing, and unforgettable memories.

LEARNING OBJECTIVES

- Use language in formal interaction with unknown people
- Understand announcements in public spaces
- Talk about daily schedules
- Use vocabulary related to personal hobbies, such as music
- Understand the features of Korean music concert culture

GRAMMAR FOCUS

- −습니다/ㅂ니다
- −지만

KEY GRAMMAR AND EXPRESSIONS

1. –습니다/ㅂ니다

• **MEANING AND USAGE**

-습니다/ㅂ니다 is attached to the base of action and descriptive verbs, and it indicates a formal speech level. In other words, it is used instead of -아/어요 to increase the level of formality of the speech. The choice to use -습니다/ㅂ니다 depends on the relationship between speaker and hearer, and the formality of the situation. -습니다/ㅂ니다 is used, for example, when speaking in front of an audience, by TV news anchors, and in formal settings.

• **STRUCTURE**

-습니다 is attached to the base of verbs ending in consonants, including the past tense ending. -ㅂ니다 is attached to the base of verbs ending in vowels. If used in the interactive sentences, they change respectively into -습니까?/-ㅂ니까?

가다 ➡ 가 + ㅂ니다 ➡ 갑니다
갔어요 ➡ 갔 + 습니다 ➡ 갔습니다
걷다 ➡ 걷 + 습니다 ➡ 걷습니다
걸었어요 ➡ 걸었 + 습니다 ➡ 걸었습니다
하다 ➡ 하 + ㅂ니다 ➡ 합니다
했어요 ➡ 했 + 습니다 ➡ 했습니다

• **EXAMPLES**

여러분, 안녕하십니까? KBS 9시 뉴스입니다. K팝에 대한 뉴스로 시작하겠습니다.

뉴스 앵커 Good evening, everyone, and welcome to KBS 9 O'Clock News. Tonight, we begin with the vibrant world of K-pop.

2. –지만

• MEANING AND USAGE

-지만 is attached to the base of processive and descriptive verbs to connect two sentences with a contrasting meaning. It is the English equivalent of "but".

• STRUCTURE

보다 is attached to all verb bases, both consonant-ending and vowel-ending.

받다 ➡ 받 + 지만 ➡ 받지만
먹다 ➡ 먹 + 지만 ➡ 먹지만
하다 ➡ 하 + 지만 ➡ 하지만

• EXAMPLES

이 스키장은 숙박 시설이 좋지만 조금 비싸요.
➡ This ski resort has good accommodation facilities, but it's a bit expensive.

저는 인디 밴드 음악은 많이 듣지만 대중 가요는 잘 안 들어요.
➡ I listen to indie band music a lot, but I don't really listen to pop songs.

사랑: 타오 씨, 이번에 콘서트장에 가세요?
Tao, are you going to the concert this time?

타오: 아니요. 저도 한국에서 K팝 콘서트를 보러 가고 싶었지만 티켓을 못 구했어요.
No. I also wanted to go to a K-pop concert in Korea, but I couldn't get tickets.

대화 DIALOGUE

Haru is arriving at a concert hall to see her favourite singer and is about to enter the building.

 안내 직원: 어서 오세요. 반갑습니다. 티켓 확인 도와드리겠습니다.[1]

 하루: 네? 다시 한번 말씀해 주세요.

 안내 직원: 아, 티켓 확인을 도와드리겠습니다.

 하루: 네! 여기 있습니다.

 안내 직원: 여기 이 클래퍼도 가져 가십시오.

 하루: 네. 감사합니다. 그런데 저 혹시 R석은 어느 쪽으로 가야 해요?

 안내 직원: R석은 저쪽입니다.

 하루: 감사합니다.

💬 **Role-play the dialogue by substituting the colour-coded words or phrases with the prompts below.**

 R석 — 저쪽

 굿즈 부스 — 콘서트장 밖

 매점 — 왼쪽

 화장실 — 2층

---

1. The phrase 도와드리겠습니다 translates as "I will help you" or "let me help you," and presents a manner of speaking. Its nuance suggests a subtly decisive tone.

읽기 READING

Pre-reading Activity

Link the words on the left to the sentences on the right that explain their meanings. An example has been provided.

홍보	● 가수나 배우의 회사예요.
연습생	● 아침부터 저녁까지의 스케줄이에요.
하루 일과	● 다 같이 함께 연습해요.
단체 연습	● 아직 가수/배우가 아니에요.
개인 연습	● 혼자서 연습해요.
소속사	● 사람들한테 소개해요.

Reading Activity

Read the transcript of an idol group member's interview on a YouTube show. What do trainees need to practice every day to become singers in the future?

○○그룹의 아이돌 우주는 얼마 전 유튜브 콘텐츠에 새로운 노래를 홍보하러 나왔습니다. 거기서 옛날 연습생 때 이야기를 했습니다. 우주는 "하루에 춤과 노래를 4~5시간 연습했습니다"라고 말했습니다. 그리고 그는 연습생의 하루 일과에 대해 좀 더 많이 이야기했습니다.

"보통 연습생들은 오전 9시부터 운동을 해야 합니다. 보통 매일 2시간쯤 운동을 합니다. 가끔은 *PT도 하고 스트레칭도 많이 합니다. 그 이후에 11시부터 외국어 공부를 합니다. 그리고 1시에 점심 식사를 하고 3시부터 한 시간 동안 스피치 수업을 받습니다. 그리고 보컬과 춤 수업을 듣습니다. 그 다음에 단체 연습과 개인 연습을 밤 늦게까지 합니다. 그런데 고등학생 연습생들은 오전에는 학교에 가고 오후부터 저녁까지 소속사에서 연습을 합니다. 보통 밤 10시에 하루 일과가 끝나지만 저는 더 늦게까지 연습했습니다." 우주는 "연습생 때 많이 힘들었지만 그 연습 때문에 지금 가수가 되었습니다."라고 인터뷰를 끝냈습니다.

*personal training

READING

A. Check off the statement if it is correct.

1. 아이돌 우주는 새로운 노래를 소개하러 유튜브에 나왔습니다. ☐
2. 아이돌 우주는 보통 하루에 5시간보다 많이 연습했습니다. ☐
3. 우주는 오전에는 운동을 했지만 오후에는 개인 연습만 했습니다. ☐
4. 고등학생 연습생은 오전에는 학교에 가고 오후에는 소속사로 갑니다. ☐
5. 보통 연습생들의 하루 일과는 밤에 끝납니다. ☐

B. Answer the following questions.

1. 아이돌 우주는 왜 유튜브에 나왔습니까?

2. 연습생들은 보통 하루를 어떻게 보냅니까? (여섯 가지 활동)
   - 오전 9시 _____
   - 오전 11시 _____
   - 오후 1시 _____
   - 오후 3시 _____
   - 그리고 _____
   - 그 다음에 _____

3. Create a title for this reading material.
   _____
   _____

READING

After-reading Activity

The following schedule outlines a sample daily routine of an idol group.

1. Take turns telling your partner about each activity and its scheduled time.

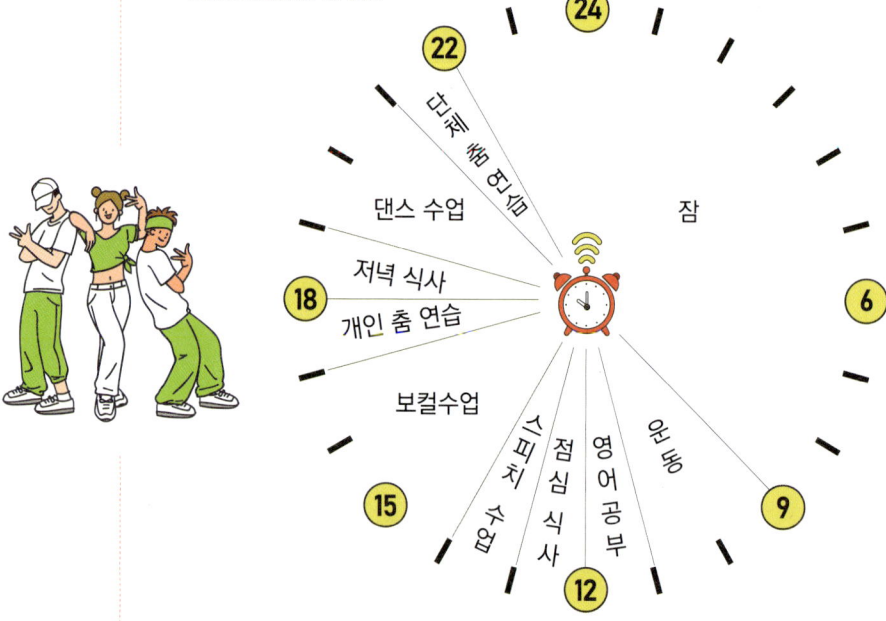

2. Now describe something that you are good at, such as a sport, an instrument, a computer game, or a language, including how many hours you spent learning it and what your routine is.

3. Interview each other about your routine activities by using the formal speech form.

인터뷰 질문	대답

Fill out the blanks in the announcements on the left, and then match each announcement with the locations where you would hear them.

1. 이 버스는 경기도 □□입니다. 안전벨트를 해 주십시오.

 ①

2. □□□을 찍을 수 없습니다. 그리고 □□□을 *SNS에 업로드 하실 수 없습니다.

*SNS: Social Network Service

 ②

3. 이번 역은 강남역입니다. 내리실 □은 오른쪽입니다.

 ③

LISTENING

Listening Activity

Haru and her mother attended the concert, where they met Caroline, who also came with her daughter. What announcements are made in the concert hall?

A. Listen to the audio and then select any correct statement.

1. 공연 중에 휴대전화로 동영상을 찍을 수 있지만 음식을 먹을 수 없어요.
2. 하루는 이 가수를 좋아해요. 그래서 콘서트를 보러 왔어요.
3. 캐롤라인은 혼자 공연을 보러 왔어요.
4. 하루는 안내 방송을 모두 들었어요.
5. 응원봉은 하루 어머니의 보물 1호예요.

B. Ask and answer the following questions with your partners.

1. 공연 중에 뭘 할 수 없습니까?
2. 캐롤라인과 하루 어머니는 공연을 보러 함께 왔습니까?
3. 캐롤라인 씨의 딸은 왜 한국에 왔습니까?
4. 하루는 어디에 갔습니까?
5. 응원봉은 누구의 보물 1호입니까?

C. 여러분의 보물 1호는 무엇입니까?

_____
_____
_____

활동 ACTIVITY

You frequently hear announcements in public areas, such as in cinemas and on public transport. Practice listening to these notices with your partner and explaining them to someone who might have missed them.

 버스 안내 방송

 이 버스는 경기도 버스입니다.
안전벨트를 해 주십시오.

E.g., A: 안내 방송을 들었어요? 무슨 내용이에요?
    B: 아, 이 버스는 경기도 버스예요. 안전벨트를 해야 해요.

 영화관 안내 방송

영화관에서는 동영상을 찍을 수 없습니다.
그리고 동영상을 개인 소셜 미디어에
업로드할 수 없습니다.

 **지하철 안내 방송**

 이번 역은 강남역입니다.
내리실 문은 오른쪽입니다.
출입문 닫습니다. 출입문 닫습니다.

"보물 1호, 응원봉"

K-Pop Concert with Light Sticks!

Korea's cheering culture is a defining feature of its entertainment and sports events.

떼창 (fanchant singing) turns concerts and games into vibrant interactive experiences where fans sing in perfect harmony with performers or players.

응원봉 (light sticks) are another iconic element, with each K-pop group having a unique design that fans wave in synchronisation during performances.

These cultural elements demonstrate the deep connection between fans and their idols or teams, creating unforgettable shared moments.

[이미지 출처: 네이버/유튜브]

K-MEDIA CORNER

K-pop's global fanbase has grown dramatically, with over 100 million fans worldwide according to the Korea Foundation's 2022 statistics. This explosive growth is reflected in K-dramas that capture the vibrant world of K-pop and its passionate fandoms. *Imitation* (이미테이션) offers an inside look at the K-pop industry, portraying the intense journey of idols as they chase fame and navigate the pressures of stardom. *Her Private Life* (그녀의 사생활) dives into the life of a devoted K-pop fan who manages her professional life alongside her obsession with an idol group, showing the depth of connection fans feel. *Lovely Runner* (선재 업고 튀어) illustrated the dynamic interaction between fans and the singer. These dramas capture the vibrant energy of Kpop concerts, the strong connection between idols and their supporters, and the role of music as a universal unifying force.

 How do dramas like *Imitation* highlight the challenges of becoming a K-pop star?

 What insights do K-dramas offer about the impact of K-pop on fans and the unique relationship between idols and their followers?

[이미지 출처: 네이버/유튜브]

실제 표현
Real Expressions

- 티켓 확인 도와드리겠습니다.
→ We will assist you in checking your tickets.

- 클래퍼 하나 챙겨 드릴게요.
→ We will supply you with a clapper.

[공연 중 주의 사항] Safety Protocols During the Performance

- 객석 내부 음식물 섭취 불가
→ No food or beverages are allowed in the auditorium.

- 의자 이동 및 좌석 이탈 시, 즉시 퇴장
→ Changing or vacating seats will lead to immediate dismissal.

- 촬영 기기 적발 시 즉시 퇴장
→ Using cameras will lead to immediate dismissal.

☑ Now I know these!
Mark off what you learnt (grammar, vocabulary, usage)

- 티켓 확인 도와드리겠습니다. ☑
- 하루 일과 ☐
- 단체 연습 ☐
- 그 때는 힘들었지만 지금은 괜찮습니다. ☐
- 공연 ☐
- 응원봉 ☐
- 보물 1호 ☐

05과

감기 조심하세요!

Sarang, feeling unwell after travelling, visits a doctor. During her visit, she is asked various questions for her diagnosis. This scenario highlights essential Korean phrases that friends can use when in need in Korea.

LEARNING OBJECTIVES

- Explain reasons and causes
- Talk about basic symptoms and remedies
- Understand concrete information
- Use vocabulary related to personal health

GRAMMAR FOCUS

- –아/어서(이유)
- –(으)ㄴ 후에

KEY GRAMMAR AND EXPRESSIONS

1. –아/어서(이유)

• **MEANING AND USAGE**

-아/어서 is attached to the base of action and descriptive verbs to connect two sentences. What is described in the first sentence is the reason for what happens in the second sentence.

- -아/어서 is used when the consequence is objective and obvious.
- -아/어서 cannot be used to connect two sentences if the second sentence expresses a request or an order.
- -아/어서 cannot be attached to past tense bases (see also –(으)니까, Unit 9).

• **STRUCTURE**

-아서 is attached to verb bases containing ㅏ or ㅗ, while -어서 is attached to verb bases containing other vowels. 하다 becomes 해서.

받다 ➡ 받 + 아서 ➡ 받아서

먹다 ➡ 먹 + 어서 ➡ 먹어서

하다 ➡ 하 + 여서 ➡ 해서

• **EXAMPLES**

새 핸드폰을 생일 선물로 받아서 너무 기뻤어요.
➡ I was so happy when I got a new mobile phone for my birthday.

음식을 잘못 먹어서 배탈이 났어요.
➡ I had an upset stomach because I ate the wrong food.

지난주에 감기에 걸려서 너무 아팠어요.
➡ I caught a cold last week and was very sick.

이 제품은 디자인이 예뻐서 인기가 많아요.
➡ This product is popular because it has a beautiful design.

날씨가 좋아서 오늘 한강 공원에서 자전거를 탈 거예요.
➡ The weather is nice, so I'm going to ride my bike in Han River Park today.

안내원: 예약하셨어요?
Do you have an appointment?

하루: 아니요.
No.

안내원: 지금 사람이 많**아서** 조금 기다리셔야 해요.
There are a lot of people right now, so you will have to wait a while.

우미드: 우리 점심을 밖에서 먹을까요?
Shall we eat out for lunch?

회사 동료: 아, 우미드 씨. 저는 요즘 미국에 여행 가고 싶어서 돈을 아끼고 있어요. 그래서 도시락을 가져왔어요.
I'm sorry, Umid. I've been saving money lately because I want to travel to the US, so I brought a packed lunch.

2. -(으)ㄴ 후에

• **MEANING AND USAGE**

-(으)ㄴ 후에 is attached to the base of action verbs to indicate a temporal succession, i.e. what is described in the second sentence happens after what is described in the first sentence.

• **STRUCTURE**

-은 후에 is attached to verb bases ending with a consonant, while -ㄴ 후에 is attached to verb bases ending with a vowel.

받다 ➡ 받 + 은 후에 ➡ 받은 후에
마시 ➡ 마시 + ㄴ 후에 ➡ 마신 후에
운동하다 ➡ 운동하 + -ㄴ 후에 ➡ 운동한 후에

• EXAMPLES

운동한 후에 꼭 스트레칭을 해야 해요.
→ You must stretch after exercising.

하루: 금요일 저녁에 뭐 했어요?
What did you do on Friday evening?

우미드: 회사에 다녀온 후에 너무 피곤해서 잠만 잤어.
I was so tired after work that I just slept.

사랑: 부엌을 사용한 후에 꼭 청소해 주세요.
Please clean the kitchen after you use it.

손님: 네. 알겠어요.
Yes. Okay.

마두카: 여행 사진하고 동영상을 찍은 후에 SNS에 올리고 있어요.
I take pictures and videos of my trip and post them on social media.

우미드: 우와! 마두카 씨 동영상을 진짜 잘 찍어요! 다큐멘터리 같아요.
Wow, Maduka, your videos are really good! They're like documentaries.

대화 DIALOGUE

Maduka feels unwell, so he is seeing a doctor now.

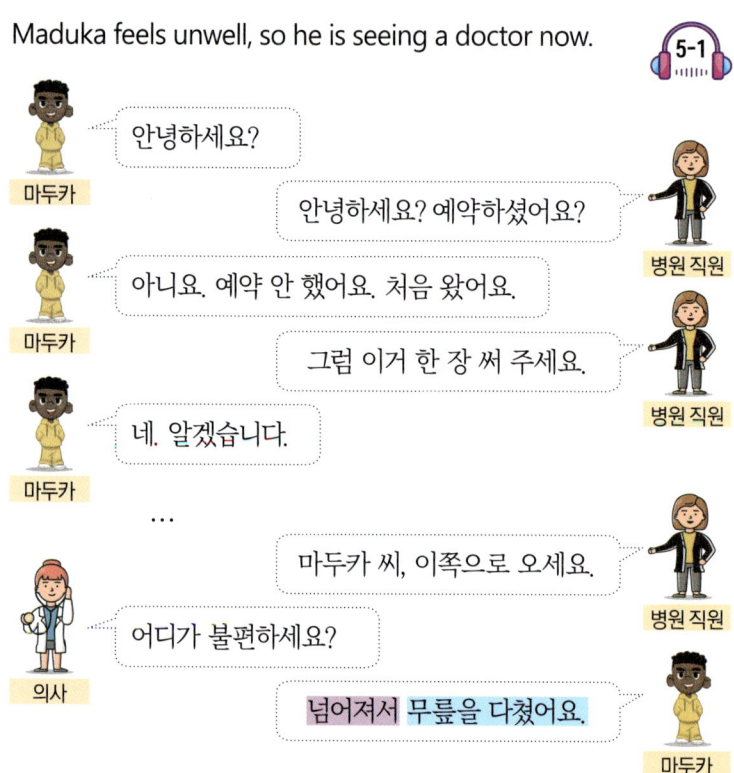

마두카: 안녕하세요?
병원 직원: 안녕하세요? 예약하셨어요?
마두카: 아니요. 예약 안 했어요. 처음 왔어요.
병원 직원: 그럼 이거 한 장 써 주세요.
마두카: 네. 알겠습니다.
…
병원 직원: 마두카 씨, 이쪽으로 오세요.
의사: 어디가 불편하세요?
마두카: 넘어져서 무릎을 다쳤어요.

💬 Role-play the dialogue by substituting the colour-coded words or phrases with the prompts below.

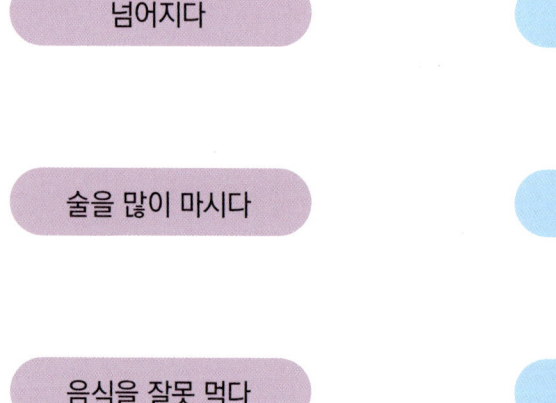

넘어지다	무릎을 다치다
술을 많이 마시다	속이 아프다
음식을 잘못 먹다	배탈이 나다
잠을 잘못 자다	목이 안 돌아가다

읽기 READING

 Pre-reading Activity

Read the list of words below, then complete the blanks in the following sentences.

E.g., 놀랐어요   감기약   닦았어요   부끄러웠어요
        약사   증상   짜증을 냈어요

1. 프리야 씨는 큰 소리에 깜짝 놀랐어요.
2. 가브리엘 씨는 코가 많이 막히고 목이 아팠어요.
   이런 감기 _____을/를 의사에게 말했어요.
3. 친구한테 거짓말을 했어요. 그런데 친구가 그것을 알았어요.
   그래서 자신이 너무 _____.
4. 남자 친구와 오늘 헤어졌어요. 그리고 버스를 탔어요. 버스에서 너무 슬퍼서 갑자기 눈물이 나왔지만 빨리 눈물을 _____.
5. _____이/가 좋은 비타민 브랜드를 추천해 줬어요.
6. 감기에 걸려서 _____을/를 사러 약국에 갔어요.
7. 동생이 너무 시끄러워서 집에서 공부를 잘 못했어요.
   그래서 동생한테 _____.

 Reading Activity

Sarang is reading a short story in an essay magazine. Why does the protagonist of the story feel ashamed?

약사와 아이

지난주 어느 날, 감기약을 사러 약국에 갔습니다. 약사에게 감기 증상을 이야기하고 있었습니다. 그때 다섯 살 쯤의 어린이가 약국에 들어왔습니다.

그리고 그 어린이가 약사한테 500원을 줬습니다. 어린이가 약사한테 이렇게 말했습니다.

"엄마가 아파요…". 그리고 갑자기 어린이가 울었습니다.

약사는 조금 놀랐습니다. 그리고 어린이한테 이렇게 말했습니다.

"엄마! 어디가, 어떻게 아파요? 이렇게 엄마한테 물어봐요. 그럼 약을 줄 수 있어요. 엄마가 약을 먹으면 빨리 나을 거예요." 그 이야기를 듣고 어린이는 눈물을 닦았습니다.

그리고 약국을 나갔습니다. 어린이가 나간 후에 약사가 저에게 말했습니다.

"아이가 참 대단해요. 엄마를 걱정해서 약국에 왔어요."

이것을 보고 며칠 전 일이 생각났습니다.

_____

그 아이를 보고 제 자신이 부끄러웠습니다.

READING

A. Together with your classmates, answer the following questions.

1. 이 사람은 왜 약국에 갔습니까?
2. 어린이는 왜 울었습니까?
3. 약사는 어린이한테 무슨 말을 했습니까?
4. 약사는 어린이를 어떻게 생각합니까?
5. 이 사람은 어린이를 보고 무슨 생각을 했습니까?

B. Write one or two sentences to complete the story.

After-reading Activity

Look at the following images, and try to narrate a story using all of them.

Have you ever felt unwell while travelling? First, complete the table below with your information, then share a brief story recounting a time when you felt unwell with your partner.

질문	내 이야기	친구 이야기
1. 언제 아팠어요?		
2. 어디에서 아팠어요?		
3. 뭐 때문에 아팠어요?		
4. 약을 먹은 후에 어떻게 됐어요?		

Pre-listening Activity

What questions do you get asked from a doctor when you are sick?

☑ 어디가 어떻게 아프세요?
☐ _____
☐ _____
☐ _____

Listening Activity

Sarang went to the hospital to see a doctor because she was experiencing a stomach ache and a fever. What are her symptoms?

A. Listen to the audio and then select any correct statement.

1. 사랑 씨는 배는 많이 아팠지만 열은 많이 안 났어요. ☐
2. 사랑 씨는 지난주 목요일부터 배가 아팠어요. ☐
3. 사랑 씨는 밥을 먹은 후에는 덜 아팠어요. ☐
4. 사랑 씨는 소화제를 먹은 후에 잠을 많이 자서 조금 괜찮아졌어요. ☐
5. 사랑 씨 가족들은 안 아파요. ☐

LISTENING

B. Ask and answer the following questions with your partners.

1. 사랑 씨는 왜 병원에 왔어요?

2. 사랑 씨는 밥을 먹은 후에 더 아팠어요? 얼마 동안 아팠어요?

3. 사랑 씨는 왜 지난주에 바로 병원에 못 왔어요?

4. 사랑 씨 가족들도 지금 아파요?

C. 사랑 씨는 의사 선생님을 만나고 왔어요. 사랑 씨는 이제 어떻게 해야 해요?

☐ _____

☐ _____

☐ _____

☐ _____

☐ _____

When you visit a clinic for the first time, you need to fill out the form regarding your information and return it to the reception desk.

Here is a sample clinic registration form. First, check the vocabulary and then fill out the form. After that, create your own mini-dialogue with your partner by taking on the roles of receptionist and patient (refer to the main dialogue).

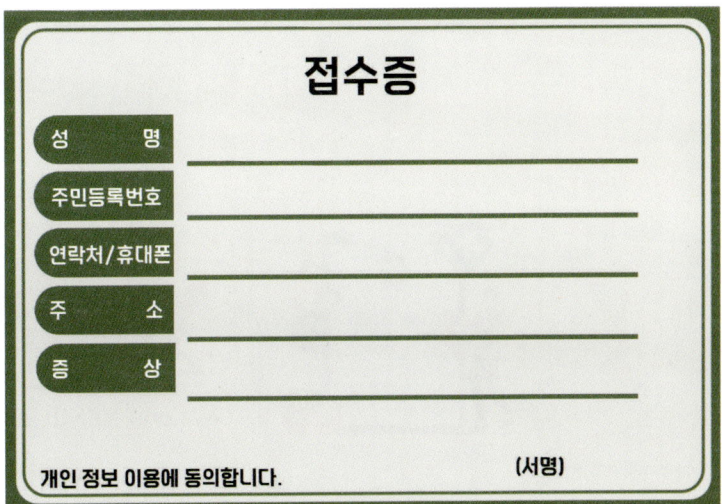

"감기 조심하세요!"

Korean Healthcare System

Korea's healthcare system, implemented nationwide by the late 1980s, offers widespread coverage and relatively affordable services, attracting medical tourists for everything from check-ups to specialised procedures. Preventive care is also common, with regular screenings seen as a key to overall well-being.

However, high-cost treatments-especially for serious conditions like cancer-aren't always fully covered, creating financial strain and heightening inequalities between the rich and poor. Recent medical strikes, sparked by policy changes and workload concerns, highlight ongoing challenges within the system.

K-MEDIA CORNER

Medical dramas in Korea often provide an engaging glimpse into the healthcare system, blending personal stories with medical challenges. *Hospital Playlist* (슬기로운 의사생활) showcases the daily lives of doctors who balance their intense medical careers with personal friendships, highlighting the warmth and dedication found in Korean hospitals.

Doctor Romantic (낭만닥터 김사부) focuses on a passionate and unconventional doctor who teaches the value of empathy and skill in medicine, showing how healthcare goes beyond treatments and deeply affect lives. *Life* (라이프) offers a more intense view of hospital politics and the moral dilemmas faced by medical professionals, emphasizing the complexities within the healthcare system.

 How do K-dramas like *Hospital Playlist* and *Doctor Romantic* portray the human side of healthcare in Korea?

 What insights into Korean healthcare and culture can we gain from medical dramas, and how do they reflect real-life experiences for patients?

[이미지 출처: 네이버/유튜브]

실제 표현
Real Expressions

- 이 진료/초진 접수증을 작성하셔서 저한테 주세요.
→ Please complete this consultation form and return it to me.

- 어디가 불편해서 오셨어요?
→ What brings you here today?

- 약을 처방해 드릴게요.
→ I will write you a prescription.

- 개인 정보 이용에 동의합니다.
→ I consent to the use of my personal information.

[증상 Symptom]

- 목에 담이 걸렸어요. → I have a crick in my neck/my neck is stiff.
- 벌에 쏘였어요. → I was stung by a bee.
- 발목을 삐었어요. → I sprained my ankle.
- 손이 데였어요. → I burned my hand.
- 손목에 금이 갔어요. → I cracked my wrist.
- 식중독에 걸렸어요. → I got food poisoning.
- 피부에 두드러기가 났어요. → I got a rash on my skin.

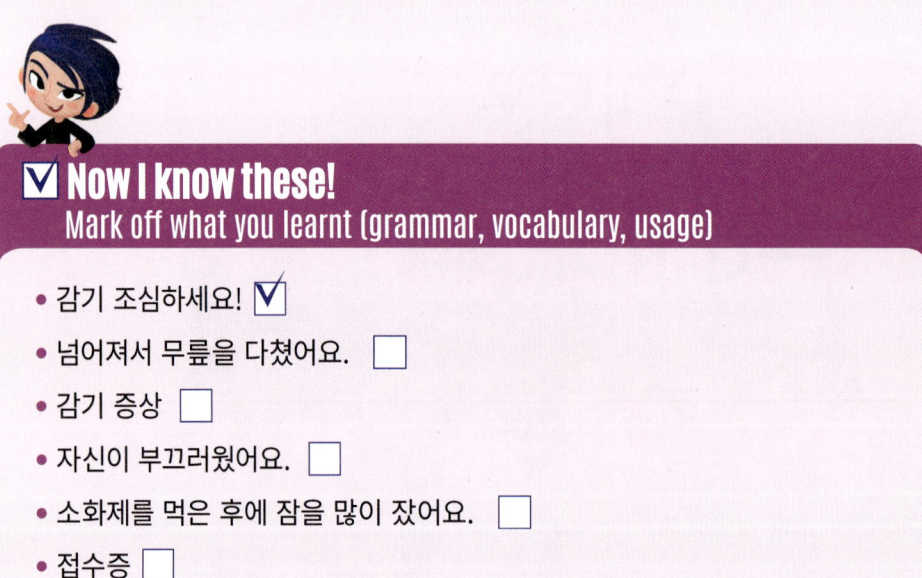

✓ Now I know these!
Mark off what you learnt (grammar, vocabulary, usage)

- 감기 조심하세요! ✓
- 넘어져서 무릎을 다쳤어요. ☐
- 감기 증상 ☐
- 자신이 부끄러웠어요. ☐
- 소화제를 먹은 후에 잠을 많이 잤어요. ☐
- 접수증 ☐

06과

까치 까치 설날은

During national holidays like the Lunar New Year, many Koreans return to their hometowns. Meanwhile, friends at a guesthouse plan their unique celebrations for New Year's Day. Discover their plans!

LEARNING OBJECTIVES

- Express an intention to do something
- Discuss plans for upcoming activities
- Use vocabulary related to holidays and festivities
- Understand the main features of the Korean holiday, the Lunar New Year

GRAMMAR FOCUS

- –(으)려고 하다
- –거나
- –(이)나

KEY GRAMMAR AND EXPRESSIONS

1. -(으)려고 하다

• **MEANING AND USAGE**

-(으)려고 indicates the intention of doing an action in the future. In this unit, it is presented as –(으)려고 하다, but it can also be followed by any other action verb (see Unit 10). It cannot occur with commands or suggestions.

• **STRUCTURE**

-으려고 하다 is attached to verb bases ending with a consonant, -려고 하다 is attached to verb bases ending with a vowel.

만나다 ➡ 만나 + 려고 해요 ➡ 만나려고 해요
먹다 ➡ 먹 + 으려고 해요 ➡ 먹으려고 해요
공부하다 ➡ 공부하 + 려고 해요 ➡ 공부하려고 해요
만들다 ➡ 만들 + 려고 해요 ➡ 만들려고 해요

• **EXAMPLES**

저는 이번 설 연휴에는 음식을 많이 안 먹으려고 해요.
➡ I'm not going to eat much during this Lunar New Year holiday.

가브리엘 씨는 건축을 공부해요. 10년 후에 멋있는 집을 지으려고 해요.
➡ Gabriel is studying architecture. He plans to build a beautiful house in ten years.

우미드 씨는 오늘부터 담배를 안 피우려고 해요.
➡ Umid is going to quit smoking starting today.

소피아 씨는 갑자기 일이 생겨서 비행기표를 취소하려고 했지만 못 했어요.
➡ Sophia suddenly had something come up, so she tried (intended) to cancel her plane ticket but couldn't.

사랑: 안녕하세요? 어서 오세요.
Hello. Please come in.

손님: 안녕하세요? 저... 체크인 하려고 해요.
Hello? I'm here to check in.

지나쌤: 캐롤라인 선생님, 이번에 한국에서 뭐 하실 거예요?
Caroline, what are you going to do in Korea this time?

캐롤라인: 이번에는 한국 문화 책을 한 권 쓰려고 해요.
This time, I'm going to write a book about Korean culture.

2. –거나

• **MEANING AND USAGE**

-거나 is attached to the base of action and descriptive verbs to indicate an alternative or an option. It has the meaning of "(doing this) or (doing that)", "(being like this) or (being like that)".

• **STRUCTURE**

-거나 is attached the all verb bases.

보다 ➡ 보 + 거나 ➡ 보거나
찍다 ➡ 찍 + 거나 ➡ 찍거나
하다 ➡ 하 + 거나 ➡ 하거나

• **EXAMPLES**

주말에는 보통 테니스를 치거나 책을 읽어요.
➡ On weekends, I usually play tennis or read books.

아파요? 그럼 약을 먹거나 병원에 꼭 가세요.
➡ Are you feeling unwell? If so, take some medicine or be sure to go to the hospital.

이 사이트에서는 물건을 사거나 팔 수 있어요.
➡ You can buy or sell items on this website.

우미드: 무슨 일 있어?
What's up?

소피아: 나 프랑스에 가야 하는데 갑자기 일이 생겼어. 그래서 비행기 표를 취소하거나 날짜를 변경해야 해.
I have to go to France, but something came up suddenly. So I have to cancel my flight ticket or change the date.

3. -(이)나

• MEANING AND USAGE

-(이)나 is a particle, attached to nouns, indicating an alternative or an option.

• STRUCTURE

-이나 is attached to nouns ending with a consonant, while 나 is attached to nouns ending with a vowel.

만두 + 나 ➡ 만두나
떡국 + 이나 ➡ 떡국이나

• EXAMPLES

명절에 떡국이나 송편을 먹어요.
➡ We eat tteokguk or songpyeon on holidays.

이번 템플스테이에서 윷놀이나 공기놀이를 다 같이 할 거예요.
➡ In this templestay, we will play yunnori or gonggi together.

대화 DIALOGUE

Sarang and Caroline discuss their Lunar New Year's holiday plans in the living room.

 캐롤라인: 사랑 씨는 이번 설 연휴에 뭐 할 거예요?

 사랑: 이번에는 제주도 할머니 댁에 가요. 거기서 차례를 지내려고 해요. 캐롤라인 씨는요?

 캐롤라인: 저는 아직 계획이 없어요.

 사랑: 그럼 제주도 할머니 댁에 같이 가실래요? 제가 할머니한테 물어볼게요.

 캐롤라인: 네. 좋아요.

Role-play the dialogue by substituting the colour-coded words or phrases with the prompts below.

차례¹를 지내다

떡국을 먹다

친척들하고 윷놀이²를 하다

할머니와 친척들에게 세배³를 하다

---

1 차례 is a Korean ritual in which families present food to their ancestors during holidays such as the Lunar New Year.

2 윷놀이 is a traditional Korean New Year game where players throw four sticks and move their pieces on a board.

3 세배 is a respectful bow to elders during the Lunar New Year.

읽기 READING

Pre-reading Activity

Read the news article about templestay programs during the Lunar New Year's holiday. What kind of experience can people have at a temple? Where can people get detailed information?

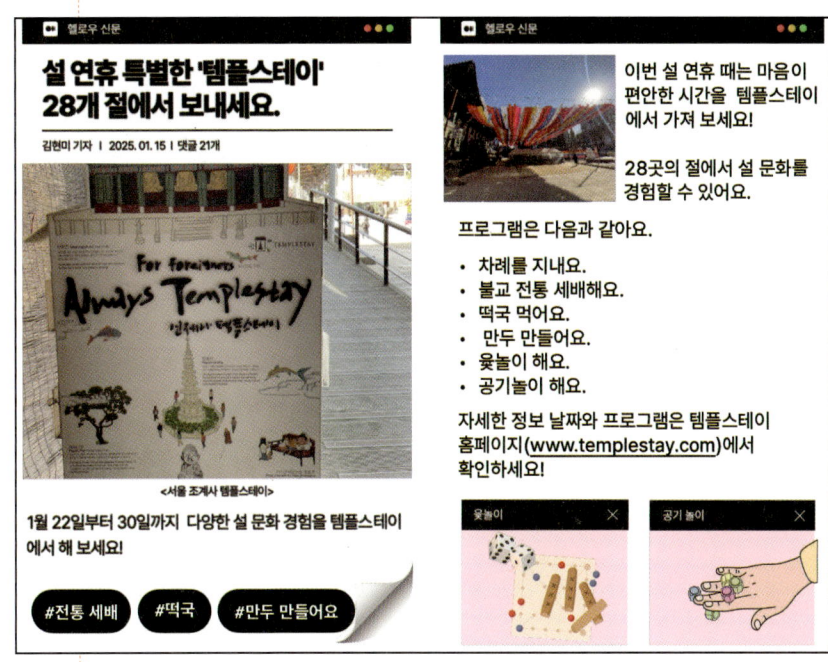

Reading Activity

Umid reads the news article about the templestay's Lunar New Year's holiday program. Here is his blog where he writes about his life in Korea. What's his plan for the Lunar New Year's holiday?

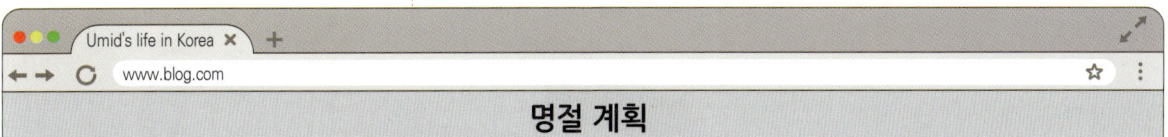

명절 계획

명절에는 가족들을 만나거나 쉴 수 있어요. 하지만 한국 친척들이 "취직했어?", "언제 결혼할 거야?", "여자 친구 있어?" 이런 것들을 자꾸 물어 봐서 가끔 스트레스를 받아요. 그리고 지난 명절 때 게스트하우스 친구 샘이 "가족이 멀리 있어서 조금 외로워요"라고 말했어요.
그래서 이번 설 연휴에 다른 계획을 세우려고 했어요. 그런데 한국에서 설 연휴 때는 많은 가게들이 문을 닫아요. 얼마 전에 신문에서 설 연휴 '템플스테이' 기사를 읽었어요. 그래서 템플스테이 홈페이지에서 정보를 찾아 봤어요. 프로그램이 너무 마음에 들어서 이번 명절에 템플스테이에 가기로 했어요. 여러 절 중에서 서울에서 조금 가까운 공주 마곡사로 결정했어요. 마곡사 프로그램이 헬로우 신문에 있는 프로그램하고 똑같아요.
절에서 설 문화를 경험할 수 있고 친구랑 함께 갈 수 있어서 너무 신나요!!
그리고 샘과 저는 절 음식에 관심이 많아서 음식도 너무 기대돼요.

READING

A. Together with your classmates, answer the following questions.

1. 명절에 친척들이 어떤 것을 물어 봐요?
2. 템플스테이 프로그램이 어때요?
3. 우미드 씨는 여러 절 중에서 왜 마곡사로 결정했어요?
4. 마곡사 설 연휴 템플스테이 프로그램은 뭐예요?
5. 우미드 씨는 지금 기분이 어때요? 왜요?
6. 샘과 우미드 씨는 무엇에 관심이 많아서 템플스테이가 기대돼요?

B. 우미드 씨는 왜 이번 설 연휴에 다른 계획을 세우려고 했어요?

1. _____

2. _____

After-reading Activity

Look at the images on Umid's blog; Umid and Sam experienced those activities during their templestay trip over the holidays. Create a story about their trip by looking at the pictures below. Share the story you created with your partner.

 **Pre-listening Activity**

Connect the words and expressions in the box below to their meanings, as shown in the example.

> 설, 연휴, 이동하다, 고향,
> 대중교통, 이용하다, 1박 2일, 반 이상

"올해의 시작이에요." _____설_____

"여기서부터 저기까지 가요." _____

"이것을 써요." _____

"기차, 버스, 비행기, 택시, 트램, 지하철" _____

"여행 가요. 거기서 하룻밤을 자요." _____

"여기서 태어나고 자랐어요." _____

"50% 보다 많아요." _____

"이 날은 학교/ 회사에 안 가요. 집에서 쉬어요." _____

UNIT 6_ 까치 까치 설날은 **101**

LISTENING

Listening Activity

Umid and Sam are returning to the guesthouse after experiencing a templestay. While travelling back, they see the the news on TV at Seoul Station. What news are they watching? What is it about?

A. Listen to the audio file and then select any correct statement.

1. 이번 설 연휴는 작년보다 사람들이 많이 이동했어요. ☐
2. 이번 설 연휴는 27일부터 31일까지였어요. ☐
3. 대한민국 인구의 반 이상의 사람들이 고향에 가거나 여행을 갔어요. ☐
4. 교통수단으로 개인 차를 제일 많이 이용했어요. ☐
5. 가장 많은 사람들이 고향에서 1박 2일 동안 있었어요. ☐

B. Ask and answer the following questions with your partners.

1. 어떤 대중교통을 사람들이 제일 많이 이용했어요? 그 다음은요?
2. 서울에서 강릉까지는 차로 몇 시간 정도 걸렸어요?
3-1. 설 연휴 동안 몇 퍼센트의 사람들이 여행을 갔다 왔어요?
3-2. 그 중에서 해외 여행은 몇 퍼센트였어요?

C. 여러분 나라에서는 사람들이 보통 설 연휴에 고향에 가요? 거기서 가족과 함께 시간을 보내요? 아니면 여행을 가요?

활동 ACTIVITY

When is your country's most important public holiday? How long does it last? What do you usually do during that holiday? Write down your answer using the -거나 grammar structure and then discuss it with your partner.

우리 나라에서는 새해에 사람들이 보통 파티를 하거나 친구들과 같이 술 마시고 놀아요.

_____
_____
_____
_____
_____

Prompt questions:

1. 여러분 나라에서 제일 중요한 명절이 뭐예요?
2. 보통 연휴는 며칠 동안이에요?
3. 연휴 때 사람들이 보통 뭐 하려고 해요?
4. 여러분은 연휴 때 뭐 하세요?
5. 한국 설 연휴에는 가게들이 많이 문을 닫아요. 여러분은 어떻게 할 거예요? (-(으)려고 하다)

"까치 까치 설날은"

Navigating Korean Family Titles

Korean family titles can be quite specific. For instance, words for "mother" and "father" are different from those used for a mother-in-law or father-in-law. Aunts are referred to differently depending on whether they're on one's mother's or father's side, and siblings call each other by terms like 형 (older brother, if you're male), 오빠 (older brother, if you're female), 누나 (older sister, if you're male), and 언니 (older sister, if you're female). Even grandmothers are referred to as 외할머니 from one's mother's side.

Though these titles reflect a historically larger family structure, modern shifts—such as lower birth rates—mean some distinctions are less rigid. Even so, during major holidays like Lunar New Year or Chuseok, younger generations often look up the proper terms to use with relatives.

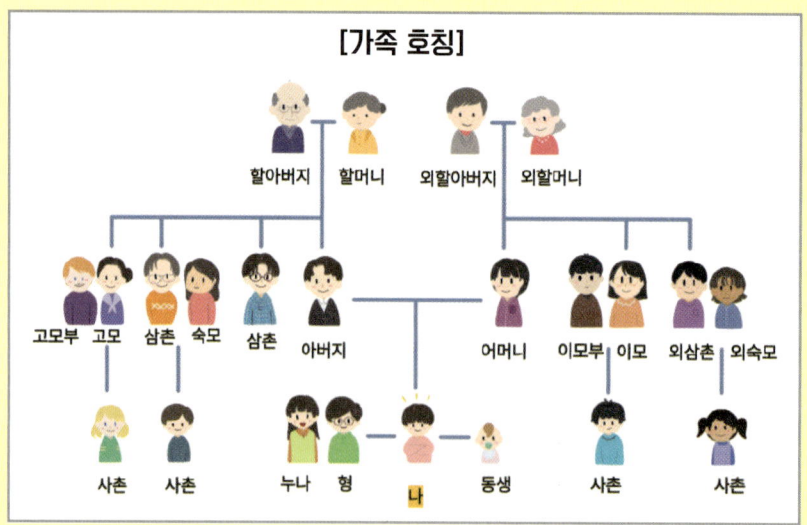

K-MEDIA CORNER

K-dramas often explore the complex dynamics of Korean family relationships, highlighting the importance of titles like 오빠, 언니, and 선배, which reflect social hierarchy and respect. *Reply 1988* (응답하라 1988) beautifully captures the intricacies of family and neighborly bonds in the 1980s, where titles and terms of address play a crucial role in daily interactions.

My Father is Strange (아버지가 이상해) dives into the lives of a close-knit family, where the use of different honorifics reflects the love, respect, and occasional conflict among siblings and parents. *Once Again* (한 번 다녀왔습니다) portrays multiple generations living together, emphasizing how titles like 할머니 (grandmother) and 삼촌 (uncle) are not just names but reflect deeper familial connections. These dramas illustrate the nuances of Korean social etiquette, showing how terms of address shape relationships, create bonds, and sometimes lead to humorous misunderstandings, much like the friends' discussion in Annyeong Korean.

 How do K-dramas like *Reply 1988* and *My Father is Strange* showcase the role of titles in shaping family dynamics in Korea?

 What can we learn about Korean social norms and respect from the way characters address each other in family-related dramas?

[이미지 출처: 네이버/유튜브]

실제 표현
Real Expressions

[신문 기사 News article]

- 설 연휴를 맞아 오는 22일부터 30일까지 전국 사찰 20여 곳에서 설 문화를 체험할 수 있는 설날 템플스테이를 운영한다고 밝혔습니다.
→ In celebration of the Lunar New Year holiday, over 20 temples across the country will offer Lunar New Year's Templestays from the 22nd to the 30th, allowing visitors to experience Lunar New Year's culture.

[출처] BBS 불교방송(https://news.bbsi.co.kr)

- 이용 교통수단은 승용차가 85.1%로 가장 많고, 버스 10.2%, 철도 3.6%, 항공기 0.7%, 여객선 0.4%로 조사됐다.
→ The most common means of transportation were private cars (85.1%), followed by buses (10.2%), trains (3.6%), airplanes (0.7%), and passenger ships (0.4%).

[출처] 대한민국 정책브리핑(www.korea.kr)

☑ Now I know these!
Mark off what you learnt (grammar, vocabulary, usage)

- 할머니 댁에서 차례를 지내려고 해요! ☑
- 세배를 해요. ☐
- 명절에는 가족들을 만나거나 쉴 수 있어요. ☐
- 새로운 계획을 세우려고 했어요. ☐
- 설 연휴 ☐
- 고향 ☐
- 1박 2일 ☐

07 과

DMZ 별다방

Gabriel's grandfather, a veteran of the Korean War, instilled in him a deep understanding of Korean history. Recently, a distinctive café has opened just 1.4 km from the North Korean border, offering visitors a chance to enjoy their coffee while reflecting on the peace between the two Koreas.

LEARNING OBJECTIVES

- Ask for people's opinions
- Ask for confirmation using tag questions
- Understand how to use online booking systems
- Use vocabulary associated with travel experiences
- Understand basic aspects of the division between South and North Korea

GRAMMAR FOCUS

- -(으)ㄹ까요?
- -지요?
- 도

KEY GRAMMAR AND EXPRESSIONS

1. -(으)ㄹ까요?

• MEANING AND USAGE

-(으)ㄹ까요? has a second meaning beyond the first meaning seen in Unit 9, volume 1. It can also be used to express a conjecture while simultaneously asking for the listener's opinion. When used this way, it is attached to the base of action and descriptive verbs.

• STRUCTURE

-을까요? is attached to verb bases ending with a consonant, while -ㄹ까요? is attached to verb bases ending with a vowel.

바쁘다 ➡ 바쁘 + ㄹ까요? ➡ 바쁠까요?
있다 ➡ 있 + 을까요? ➡ 있을까요?
하다 ➡ 하 + ㄹ까요? ➡ 할까요?

• EXAMPLES

마두카   그 공원이 여기서 가까울까요?
Do you reckon that park is close by?

가브리엘   네. 가까울 거예요.
Yes, it will be close by.

우미드   그 콘서트가 재미있을까요?
Will the concert be fun?

사랑   저는 잘 모르겠어요. 그런데 하루 씨가 그 콘서트에 갔다 왔어요. 하루 씨한테 한번 물어 보세요.
I'm not sure. But Haru went to that concert. Why don't you ask her?

소피아   사랑 씨가 왜 제주도에 안 갔을까요?
Why didn't Sarang go to Jeju Island?

타오   글쎄요.
I don't know.

가브리엘   셔틀버스는 언제 올까요?
When will the shuttle bus arrive?

안내원   금방 와요. 여기서 조금만 기다리세요.
It'll be here soon. Please wait here for a moment.

2. -지요?

• **MEANING AND USAGE**

-지요? is attached to action, descriptive verbs, and 이다 to ask about something the speaker already knows, in order to seek confirmation. It is the equivalent of saying "right?" or "isn't it?" at the end of a sentence. This kind of question is called a tag question.

• **STRUCTURE**

-지요? is attached to the base of verbs ending in both consonants and vowels. -이지요? is attached to nouns ending with consonants, while simply -지요? is attached to nouns to nouns ending with vowels. -죠 is a shortened form of 지요.

보다 ➡ 가깝 + 지요? ➡ 가깝지요?
예쁘다 ➡ 예쁘 + 지요? ➡ 예쁘지요?
군인이다 ➡ 군인 + 이지요? ➡ 군인이지요?
버스 ➡ 버스 + 지요? ➡ 버스지요?

• **EXAMPLES**

사랑: 어제 날씨가 너무 추웠지요?
Wasn't it so cold yesterday?

프리야: 네. 바람도 엄청 불고 눈도 많이 왔어요.
Yes. The wind was blowing hard and it snowed a lot.

샘: 배부르지?
You're full, aren't you?

소피아: 어. 어떻게 알았어?
Yes. How did you know?

샘: 지금 내가 혼자 다 먹고 있잖아.
Because I'm eating all of it by myself.

우미드: 샘 씨도 템플스테이에 같이 갈 거죠?
Are you going to the templestay too?

샘: 그럼요. 지금 너무 기대돼요.
Yes. I'm really looking forward to it.

3. 도

• MEANING AND USAGE

도 is a particle attached to nouns to indicate an addition. It is used to express the meaning of "also", "too". If used with negative verbs, it indicates the meaning of not even. This particle can also be used in the pattern ...도 ...도 to list similar items or actions.

• STRUCTURE

도 is attached to both nouns ending with consonants and nouns ending with vowels.

친구 + 도 ➡ 친구도
생일 ➡ 생일 + 도 ➡ 생일도
구경하다 ➡ 구경도 하다 ➡ 구경도 해요

• EXAMPLES

저도 베트남 사람이에요.
➡ I am also Vietnamese.

저는 잡채도 비빔밥도 다 잘 먹어요.
➡ I like both japchae and bibimbap.

샘 씨가 스키도 스노우보드도 잘 타요.
➡ Sam can ski and snowboard well.

제 친구를 10년만에 봤어요. 그런데 얼굴이 하나도 안 변했어요.
➡ I saw my friend for the first time in ten years. But he hasn't changed a bit.

우미드

이 식당 음식은 다 맛있어요. 반찬도 찌개도 다 너무 맛있어요.
The food at this restaurant is all delicious. The side dishes and stews are all very tasty.

사랑

그렇죠?
Right?

타오

사람들이 왜 평화 공원에 많이 갈까요?
Why do people visit this Peace Park so often?

지나쌤

재미도 있고 특별한 경험도 할 수 있어서요.
It's enjoyable, and people can have special experiences.

대화 DIALOGUE

Maduka recently read a news article about a newly opened café and shared the news with Gabriel.

 마두카: 이 카페 사진 봤어요? 북한에서 가까운 곳에 카페가 생겼어요. 카페에서 북한이 보여요.

 가브리엘: 아니요. 못 봤어요. 서울에서 가까워요?

 마두카: 네. 서울에서 갈 수 있어요.

 가브리엘: 그런데 대중교통으로 갈 수 있을까요?

 마두카: 네. 갈 수 있어요! 그런데 시간이 좀 걸려요.

💬 Role-play the dialogue by substituting the colour-coded or phrases with the prompts below.

> 대중교통으로 갈 수 있을까요?

> 시간이 얼마나 걸릴까요?

> 위험할까요?

> 한국인도 갈 수 있을까요?

읽기 READING

Pre-reading Activity

The images below represent key content from an article in Gabriel's architecture newsletter. Look at the images and engage in a discussion with your classmate about the possible subject of the article.

Reading Activity

Read the following article from Gabriel's architecture newsletter subscription. What activities are available for visitors at the Aegibong Peace Ecopark?

"카페에서 1.4km는 북한"

한국에 최근 '핫'한 카페가 생겼습니다. 이 카페는 애기봉 평화공원 안에 있습니다. 이 카페에서 북한까지 거리는 1.4km입니다. 그래서 이 카페에서 북한 마을과 산을 볼 수 있고, 가끔 북한 사람도 멀리서 볼 수 있습니다.

요즘 이 카페는 젊은 사람들한테 인기가 많습니다.
그래서 이 카페가 생긴 후에 이 공원의 방문객이 많이 늘었습니다.

방문객들은 이 카페 안에서 커피도 마시고 북한 사진도 찍을 수 있습니다. 왜냐하면 카페 창문에서 북한이 잘 보이기 때문입니다.

공원에서는 다른 여러 가지 활동도 할 수 있습니다. 전시관에서는 체험 활동도 할 수 있고 전시회도 관람할 수 있습니다. 날씨가 따뜻하고 좋은 날에는 공원에서 등산도 할 수 있습니다.

READING

그렇지만 요즘 이 카페와 공원이 인기가 많아서 공원 입장 티켓을 미리 예약해야 합니다. 〈애기봉 평화공원〉 웹사이트에서 티켓을 살 수 있습니다. 티켓 가격은 3,000원입니다.

이렇게 애기봉 공원에서는 커피를 마시고 북한을 가까이에서 볼 수 있어서 방문객들이 특별한 경험을 할 수 있습니다. 그렇지만 북한이 가까워서 긴장감도 느낄 수 있습니다. 카페 방문객 중 한 명인 김미영 씨는 "한국과 북한 사이의 평화를 고민해 볼 수 있어서 여기에 왔어요."라고 말했습니다. 여러분들은 이곳에 대해 어떻게 생각하십니까? 함께 생각해 봅시다.

A. Together with your classmates, answer the following questions.

1. 북한을 볼 수 있는 카페가 어디에 있어요?

2. 이 카페에서 무엇을 할 수 있어요?

3. 이 카페는 요즘 누구한테 인기가 있어요?

4. 방문객들은 공원에서 무엇을 할 수 있어요?

5. 공원 입장 티켓은 어떻게 예약할 수 있어요? 가격은 얼마예요?

B. 뉴스레터 기사에 따르면, 방문객들은 어떤 특별한 경험을 할 수 있어요?

_____
_____

C. 카페 방문객인 김미영 씨는 무슨 말을 했어요?

_____
_____

READING

 **After-reading Activity**

You've booked an entry ticket to the Aegibong Peace Ecopark and received a confirmation text message. First, answer the questions below, then tell your partner about the message.

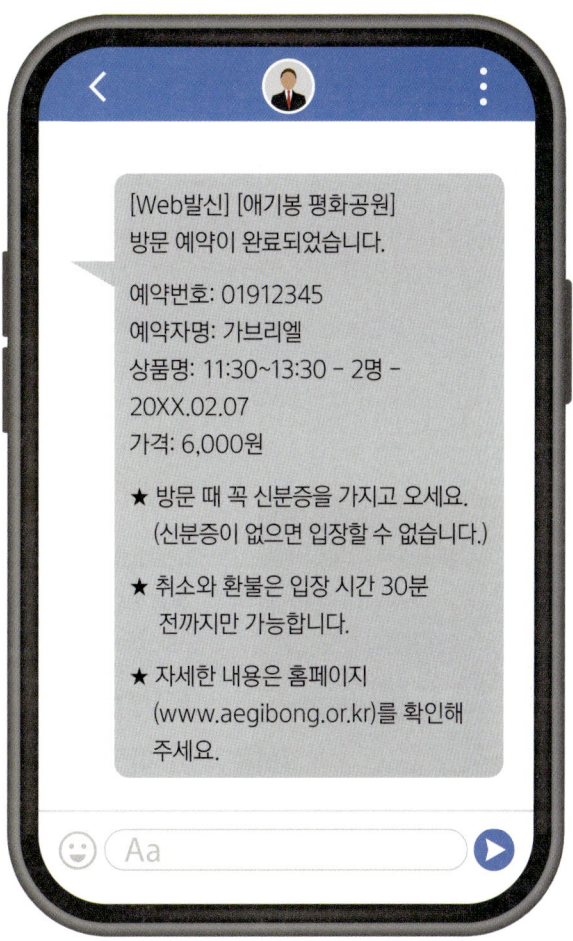

1. 예약번호가 뭐예요?
2. 티켓 가격은 얼마예요?
3. 이 공원에 갈 때 뭐 가지고 가야 해요?

듣기 LISTENING

🎧 Pre-listening Activity

Look at the image below and try to read the items on the map. Then, take on the role of a tour guide and introduce this location to your partner.

🎧 Listening Activity

Maduka and Gabriel are approaching their destination and buying tickets at the ticket office. What did the ticket seller ask them?

A. Listen to the audio file and then select any correct statement.

1. 이 공원에 가고 싶어요? 그럼 신분증이 있어야 해요. ☐
2. 티켓 검사는 셔틀버스를 탄 다음에 해요. ☐
3. 셔틀버스는 오른쪽 주차장에서 타요. ☐
4. 셔틀버스는 40분 뒤에 와요. ☐
5. 이 공원은 개인 자동차로도 셔틀버스로도 갈 수 없어요. ☐

B. Ask and answer the following questions with your partners.

1. 공원 카페는 어디에 있어요?
2. 공원 전시관은 어느 쪽에 있어요?
3. 구경을 다 한 후에 어디에서 셔틀버스를 타야 해요?

C. 셔틀버스는 몇 분마다 와요?

활동 ACTIVITY

Check the booking system below and book a ticket by selecting a date and time with your partner using the 도, -(으)ㄹ까요?, and -지요? grammar structures. After that, visit the Aegibong Peace Ecopark website (QR code) and discuss the activities you want to do with your partner.

E.g.
▶ 7일 괜찮지요?
▶ 금요일 괜찮지요?
▶ 금요일도 토요일도 다 괜찮아요.
▶ 11시 30분에는 사람이 많을까요?

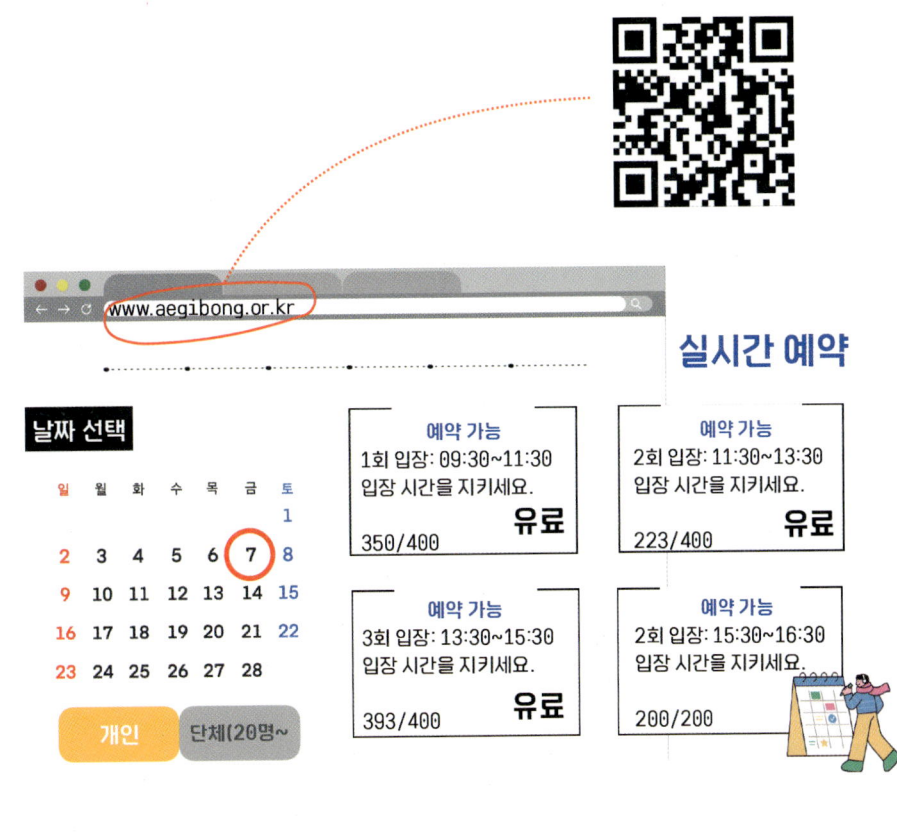

"DMZ와 별다방"

A Coffee Break at the DMZ

The Demilitarised Zone (DMZ) between North and South Korea has long stood as a symbol of the peninsula's division, now stretching over 70 years. During this time, the language and culture on each side have diverged, reflecting vastly different political and social realities. While the DMZ remains a stark reminder of family separations, many of those directly affected by the division have now passed away, leaving their stories as a legacy of a fractured history.

In November 2024, a Starbucks opened at the Aegibong Peace Ecopark in Gimpo, Gyeonggi Province, just 1.4 kilometres from North Korea. This unique location allows visitors to enjoy their coffee while gazing across the border at North Korean villages and landmarks. The café has garnered international attention, with media outlets highlighting the juxtaposition of a global coffee chain operating so close to one of the world's most secretive nations. This development adds a modern twist to a historically tense area, inviting visitors to reflect on the profound changes and enduring contrasts between the two Koreas over the past seven decades.

K-MEDIA CORNER

Dramas set around the DMZ and North Korea often explore the complex and sensitive nature of the Korean peninsula's division. **Crash Landing on You** (사랑의 불시착) is one of the most popular dramas that delves into the contrasting lives of South and North Koreans, following a South Korean heiress who accidentally lands in North Korea.

The series beautifully captures the differences and unexpected connections between people on both sides of the border. **King 2 Hearts** (더킹 투하츠) presents a fictional world where South Korea is a constitutional monarchy, exploring the tense and complicated relationship with North Korea through a royal romance. **Doctor Stranger** (닥터 이방인) showcases the life of a talented doctor who flees North Korea, highlighting the challenges and emotional struggles faced by North Korean defectors. These dramas offer viewers a glimpse into the realities and human stories surrounding the DMZ, much like the eye-opening experience of Sarang and her friends in *Annyeong? Korean!*

 How do dramas like *Crash Landing on You* portray the contrasts and unexpected connections between North and South Korea?

 What insights into the complexities of life near the DMZ and North Korea do K-dramas offer, and how do they shape viewers' understanding of the Korean divide?

[이미지 출처: 네이버/유튜브]

실제 표현
Real Expressions

[애기봉 평화생태 공원 예약 관련 Aegibong Peace Ecopark Reservation Information]

- 방문 예약이 완료되었습니다.
→ Your visit reservation has been confirmed.

- 전송된 모바일 티켓을 통해 입장 시간, 퇴장 시간을 꼭 확인해 주세요.
→ Please check your mobile ticket for entry and exit.

- 최종 퇴장 마감 시간(17:30)을 반드시 지켜주시기 바랍니다.
→ Please be sure to leave by the final exit time (17:30).

- 회차별 입장 시간을 준수해 주시기 바랍니다.
→ Please adhere to the designated entry times for each session.

- 출입 신청서 → Entry Application Form

- 서약자 대표(인솔자) → Representative (Leader)

- 이동 수단 → Mode of Transportation

☑ Now I know these!
Mark off what you learnt (grammar, vocabulary, usage)

- 대중교통으로 갈 수 있을까요? ☑
- 방문객 ☐
- 긴장감을 느끼다. ☐
- 신분증을 가지고 오셨죠? ☐
- 개인 자동차로도 셔틀버스로도 갈 수 있어요. ☐
- 30분마다 ☐

08과

떡볶이 리뷰왕

The friends watch a YouTuber review a special tteokbokki dish, which prompts them to seek out this spicy Korean comfort food known for bringing relief and joy. What comfort food makes you feel relieved right away?

LEARNING OBJECTIVES

- Explain actions and events happening in sequence
- Express a personal evaluation and personal preferences
- Use vocabulary related to street food and food deliveries
- Understand the Korean culture of food delivery and street food

GRAMMAR FOCUS

- −기 전에
- −아/어서(순차)
- 에게/한테; 에게서/한테서

KEY GRAMMAR AND EXPRESSIONS

1. -기 전에

• MEANING AND USAGE

-기 전에 is attached to the base of processive verbs to indicate that the action described in the second sentence happens before the action described in the first sentence.

• STRUCTURE

-기 전에 is attached to both verbs with bases ending with vowels and bases ending with consonants.

사다 ➡ 사 + 기 전에 ➡ 사기 전에
넣다 ➡ 넣 + 기 전에 ➡ 넣기 전에
하다 ➡ 하 + 기 전에 ➡ 하기 전에

• EXAMPLES

저는 잠을 자기 전에 핸드폰을 안 봐요.
➡ I don't use my phone before going to bed.

테니스 치기 전에 꼭 스트레칭을 해야 해요.
➡ I always stretch before playing tennis.

호주에서는 길을 건너기 전에 꼭 오른쪽을 봐야 해요. 차가 오른쪽에서 와요.
➡ In Australia, you must look right before crossing the road. Cars come from the right.

마두카: 사랑 씨, 뭐 하세요?
What are you doing, Sarang?

사랑: 지금 게스트하우스 청소하려고 해요. 이따가 손님 오기 전에 게스트하우스 방을 정리해야 해서요.
I'm cleaning the guest house. I have to tidy up the guest rooms before the guests arrive later.

가브리엘: 구름이 많네. 비가 오기 전에 빨리 가자.
There are a lot of clouds. Let's hurry before it rains.

소피아: 나 우산 있어! 천천히 가자.
I have an umbrella! Let's go slowly!

소피아: 버스에서 내리기 전에 카드를 찍으세요. 그럼 지하철을 무료로 갈아탈 수 있어요.
Tap your card before getting o the bus. Then you can transfer to the subway for free.

마두카: 알려줘서 고마워요!
Thanks for letting me know!

동료: 우미드 씨, 어디에 가요?
Umid, where are you going?

우미드: 아, 회사 들어가기 전에 커피 사려고 해요. 커피 드실래요?
Oh, I'm going to buy some coffee before going to the office. Would you like some?

동료: 네! 고마워요. 저는 아메리카노예요.
Yes, thank you. I'll have an Americano.

2. -아/어서(순차)

• MEANING AND USAGE

-아/어서, beyond expressing a reason as seen in Unit 5, can also be used to indicate a temporal sequence. Specifically, it is used to show that two actions occur one after the other in a tightly connected manner. The grammar implies that the first action is a prerequisite for the second to take place.

• STRUCTURE

-아서 is attached to verb bases containing ㅏ or ㅗ, while -어서 is attached to verb bases containing other vowels. 하다 becomes 해서.

볶다 ➡ 볶 + 아서 ➡ 볶아서

만들다 ➡ 만들 + 어서 ➡ 만들어서

하다 ➡ 하 + 여서 ➡ 해서

• EXAMPLES

지난주에 한라산 등산을 하고 싶었어요. 그래서 제주도에 갔어요. 그리고 한라산에 올라가기 전에 김밥집에 가서 김밥을 2줄 샀어요. 친구가 이 김밥집을 추천했어요. 그래서 김밥을 산 후에 한라산에 갔어요. 한라산에 올라가서 김밥을 먹었어요. 그리고 경치도 구경했어요. 그리고 산에서 내려와서 바로 근처 식당에 갔어요. 너무 배고팠어요.

➡ Last week, I wanted to climb Halla Mountain. So I went to Jeju Island. Before climbing Halla Mountain, I went to a gimbap restaurant and bought two gimbap rolls. My friend recommended this gimbap restaurant. So after buying the gimbap, I went to Halla Mountain. I ate the gimbap while climbing Halla Mountain. I also enjoyed the scenery. After descending the mountain, I went to a restaurant nearby. I was very hungry.

우미드: 오랜만에 산에 와서 다리가 좀 아파요. 여기 잠깐 앉을까요?
It's been a while since I came to the mountains, so my legs hurt a little. Shall we sit here for a moment?

타오: 네. 좋아요. 그럼 여기 앉아서 밥도 먹고 차도 마실까요?
Yes, that's a good idea. Shall we sit here and have some food and tea?

식당 주인: 소스 여기 있어요. 냉면을 잘라서 드릴까요?
Here's the sauce. Shall I cut the cold noodles for you?

타오: 아니요. 괜찮습니다. 샘 씨, 냉면에 이 소스를 좀 넣어서 드세요. 그럼 더 맛있어요!
No, that's okay. Sam, put a little of this sauce on the cold noodles. It'll taste better!

샘: 이게 무슨 소스예요?
What kind of sauce is this?

3. 에게/한테; 에게서/한테서

• MEANING AND USAGE

에게/한테 are particles attached to nouns and they are used to indicate that a certain action is directed toward a person or animal. They function similarly to the preposition "to" in English. 에게서/한테서 are also particles attached to nouns however they are used to indicate that a certain action comes from a person or animal. They function similarly to the preposition "from" in English.

• STRUCTURE

에게/한테 and 에게서/한테서 are attached to both vowel-ending and consonant-ending nouns.

친구 ➡ 친구 + 에게 ➡ 친구에게
손님 ➡ 손님 + 한테 ➡ 손님한테
누구 ➡ 누구 + 한테서 ➡ 누구한테서

• EXAMPLES

저녁 먹고 유튜브를 보고 있었어요. 그때 부모님한테서 전화를 받았어요.
➡ I was watching YouTube after dinner. Then I got a call from my parents.

소피아 씨는 유튜브 팬한테서 응원봉 선물을 받았어요.
➡ Sophia received a light stick as a gift from a YouTube fan.

마두카: 한국인에게 어떤 명절이 중요해요?
What holidays are important to Koreans?

지나쌤: 제 생각에는 설날이 제일 중요해요. 그 때는 정말 많은 사람들이 고향으로 가요.
I think New Year's Day is the most important. Many people go back to their hometowns at that time.

대화 DIALOGUE

Maduka is asking Tao which video he is watching.

마두카: 무슨 떡볶이 영상이야?

타오: 즉석 떡볶이 맛집이야.

마두카: 와, 맛있겠다! 다른 즉석 떡볶이랑 좀 달라?

타오: 응. 여기는 떡볶이에 토마토 소스하고 치즈를 넣어.

마두카: 그렇구나. 우리 저기 가서 다 같이 먹어 보자!

타오: 좋은 생각이야!

Role-play the dialogue by substituting the colour-coded words or phrases with the prompts below.

저기 가다

저거 사다

이거 만들다

이거 시키다

 Pre-reading Activity

Read the following paragraph. Then, number each ingredient in the order you would add it to the pot.

"즉석떡볶이를 더 맛있게 드시고 싶으세요?
그럼 만두, 라면, 치즈와 함께 드세요.
먼저 떡볶이를 끓인 후에 라면을 넣으세요.
그리고 치즈를 넣기 전에 만두를 먼저 넣고 2분 기다리세요.
마지막으로 치즈를 넣으세요.
그 다음에 맛있게 드세요.
그런데 아직도 배가 고프세요?
그럼 떡볶이를 다 먹은 후에 밥을 볶아서 드세요!"

A. 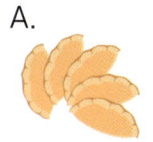   B. 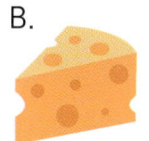   C.    D.

_____   _____   _____   _____

READING

 **Reading Activity**

Sophia has just uploaded a new episode of the Seoul Vlog on her YouTube channel. Read the comments on her video: Which menu is Sophia introducing? Also, what menus are mentioned in the comments?

💬 댓글 395개   ▶ 정렬 기준 (인기 댓글순)

H 댓글 추가…

A 즉석 떡볶이는 여기가 짱입니다. 꿀맛! 😊

B 여기 사장님이 정말 친절하세요!! 이번 주말에 또 가고 싶어요!!

C 언니! 떡볶이 리뷰 진짜 최고예요!!! 🤩

D 지난주에 여자 친구하고 한강 공원에서 데이트했어. 점심에 저 떡볶이를 배달 시켜서 먹었어 ㅋㅋㅋ 로제 떡볶이 2인분에 치즈하고 밥을 추가했어. 엄청 배불렀어.

E 소피아 언니…추천 고마워요!! 다음 에피소드도 너무 기대돼요!! ^^

F 대박! 나중에 남자 친구랑 저기 같이 가서 떡볶이 먹고 싶다!

G 오~ 소피아님! 저희 동네 오셨네요! 🎉 소피아님, 오늘도 흰 옷을 입고 떡볶이를 드셨어요?? 대박 ㅋㅋ 놀라워요!! ㅋㅋ

H 저기 엄청 맛있는데 나만 알고 싶다 ㅠㅠ 여기 국물 떡볶이가 진짜 최고입니다. 💪

I 여기 2015년도에 학교 끝나고 진짜 많이 갔었어요. 친구들과의 모임 장소예요. ㅋㅋ 다들 이거 먹으러 와서요. 이거 먹은 후에 근처 아이스크림 가게 가서 2차로 빙수 먹었는데… 옛날 생각이 나네요.

J 여기 토마토 떡볶이와 짜장 떡볶이 진짜 진짜 맛있지요…

K 저는 2주 전에 갔어요. 저는 고추장 떡볶이를 먹었어요. 저한테는 조금 매워서 치즈 추가했어요. 치즈는 맛있었지만 떡볶이는 다른 떡볶이 집하고 비슷했어요.

L 소피아 언니처럼 즉석 떡볶이 냄비에 라면을 넣고 2분만 끓이세요. 그리고 치즈를 넣고 바로 섞으세요. 여기는 치즈를 꼭 넣어서 먹어야 합니다. 그리고 볶음밥도 추가해서 꼭 드셔 보세요. 여기는 볶음밥이 필수예요.

M 이 식당 굿 👍❤️

N 오늘 친구랑 갔다 왔어요. 떡볶이 양이 적었어요. 남자 2명이 4인분 시켜서 먹었어요. 남자분들은 이렇게 드세요! 생각보다 비싸용. ㅠㅠ

O 여기 중학생 때부터 다녔어요. 단골집이에요!!!

P 여러분, 여기 근처에 신당동 떡볶이도 추천해요!! 오늘도 갔다 왔어용. ㅎㅎㅎ

READING

A. The comments are related to different aspects of Sophia's video. For each aspect, select the most appropriate comment among the three provided.

1	맛 리뷰	(A)	B	E
2	식당 추천과 먹는 방법	F	G	L
3	자기 추억/이야기	C	I	J
4	"가고 싶다/먹고 싶다"	F	K	O
5	유튜버한테 말해요	D	G	P

B. Answer the question and then ask your partner.

1. 어떤 사람들은 먹는 방법에 대해 말했어요. 이 방법이 뭐예요?

2. 어떤 사람은 떡볶이를 배달 시켜서 먹었어요. 이 사람은 뭘 주문했어요?

3. 댓글 사람들이 다 이 집 떡볶이를 좋아해요?

4. 여기 댓글 중에서 어떤 것이 마음에 들어요? 그 이유가 뭐예요?

_____
_____

READING

 **After-reading Activity**

Here are two food delivery reviews from a delivery app. Read them and discuss with your partner what they like and do not like about the food and the restaurant. What would you say to the reviewer on the delivery app if you were the owner or the chef of the restaurant?

 사장님   지난주

Look at the vocabulary and expressions below with their English translations. Then, write a mini-dialogue using the vocabulary and expressions as shown in the example.

- 소울 푸드: soul food
- 순위 (1위, 2위, 3위): ranking (1st, 2nd, 3rd)
- 정리하다: to organise/to put in order
- 주문하다: to order (food or buy something online)
- 양이 많다: the portion is large/significant.
- 추천하다: to recommend

A: 한국 사람의 소울 푸드는 뭐예요?
B: 치킨이에요.

A: 제 인생의 1순위는 돈이에요.
B: 돈이요? 돈이 제일 중요해요?
A: 네!

Listening Activity

Tao is tuning into a podcast about must-try restaurant tours. What topics does this episode cover?

A. Listen to the audio file and then select any correct statement.

1. 팟캐스트 MC 나리 씨는 요즘 맛집 책을 쓰고 있어서 즐거워요. ☐
2. 나리 씨는 힘들거나 피곤할 때 떡볶이를 먹어요. ☐
3. 사람들이 생각보다 김치찌개를 많이 안 먹어요. ☐
4. 나리 씨는 초등학교 때도 떡볶이를 먹었어요. ☐
5. 회사원들은 제육볶음을 자주 먹지 않지만 좋아해요. ☐

B. Ask and answer the following questions with your partners.

1. 나리 씨의 소울 푸드는 뭐예요? 왜 그걸 먹어요?

2. 김치찌개를 사람들이 왜 좋아해요?

3. 나리 씨는 떡볶이를 어디에 가서, 얼마나 자주 먹어요?

4. 회사원들은 왜 제육볶음을 좋아해요? (두 가지)

C. 팟캐스트에서 나리 씨는 2가지 음식을 추천했어요. 이 음식들이 뭐예요? 그리고 추천 이유가 뭐예요?

_____
_____
_____
_____

활동 ACTIVITY

Discuss with your partner your soul/comfort food by asking the questions below, and leave a review of your must-try restaurant and your favorite comfort food.

- ☑ 여러분들의 소울 푸드는 뭐예요?
- ☑ 언제 이 음식을 드세요?
- ☑ 식당에 가서 이 음식을 드세요? (식당에 가세요? 그럼 어느 식당에 가서 드세요?) 만들어서 먹어요? (그 음식을 어떻게 만들어요?)
- ☑ 여러분 나라의 소울 푸드는 뭐예요? 왜 사람들이 그 음식을 좋아해요?

▶ 여러분의 소울 푸드 맛집과 음식 리뷰를 해 주세요.
그리고 이유도 말해 주세요.

UNIT 8_ 떡볶이 리뷰왕

K-CULTURE

"떡볶이 리뷰왕"

Korea's beloved comfort food

Korea's snack culture is a nostalgic journey for its people, offering comfort and joy through iconic street foods like 붕어빵 (fish-shaped pastries) and 어묵 (fish cakes) in winter, as well as 소떡소떡 (sausage and rice cake skewers) and 호두과자 (walnut cookies) at highway rest stops.

Another beloved trio is 김밥, 떡볶이, 순대-fondly nicknamed 김떡순-a popular combination of gimbap, spicy rice cakes, and blood sausage often shared among friends after school or at bustling street markets. Many of these snacks are tied to cherished memories of family trips or school outings, reflecting the heart of Korean food culture.

The tradition of 덤 (adding extra pieces for free) further highlights the warmth and generosity of Korea's snack vendors, making every bite even more special.

K-MEDIA CORNER

떡볶이 and traditional market foods are more than just snacks in Korea-they're symbols of comfort, healing, and community. *In Mystic Pop-up Bar* (쌍갑포차), characters find solace in traditional dishes like 떡볶이, served at a magical market stall that offers both food and emotional support. *Reply 1988* (응답하라 1988) captures the heart of Korean market culture, where neighbors and friends gather around steaming pots of spicy 떡볶이, fish cakes, and other street foods, showing how these simple moments can bring people together.

The book I Want to Die But I Want to Eat Tteokbokki (죽고 싶지만 떡볶이는 먹고 싶어) reflects the deep emotional connection people have with food, especially 떡볶이, as a source of comfort during life's toughest moments. These stories highlight how traditional market foods like 떡볶이 offer not just physical nourishment but also emotional warmth, just as Sarang and her friends experience in Annyeong? Korean!

 How do dramas like *Mystic Pop-up Bar* and *Reply 1988* use traditional market food to illustrate themes of comfort and community?

 What insights about mental health and self-care can we gain from the portrayal of food in I Want to Die But I Want to Eat Tteokbokki?

실제 표현
Real Expressions

[배달 앱 - 떡볶이 리뷰 카테고리 Delivery App - Tteokbokki Review Category]

- 재주문하게 된다는 떡볶이
→ Tteokbokki that makes you want to order again.

- 맛있다는 평이 많은 떡볶이
→ Tteokbokki with numerous positive reviews.

- 깔끔한 맛이 일품인 떡볶이
→ Tteokbokki with a clean, delicious flavour.

- 매콤함이 돋보이는 떡볶이
→ Tteokbokki featuring a standout spicy taste.

- 가격 대비 우수한 떡볶이
→ Tteokbokki offering excellent value for money.

- 컨디션 업을 위한 떡볶이
→ Tteokbokki to boost your energy.

☑ Now I know these!
Mark off what you learnt (grammar, vocabulary, usage)

- 저 떡볶이집에 가서 다 같이 먹어 보자! ☑
- 치즈를 넣기 전에 만두를 먼저 넣으세요. ☐
- 소울 푸드 ☐
- 1순위 ☐
- 맛도 좋고 양도 많아요. ☐
- 시간을 아낄 수 있어요. ☐

09과

으쌰라 으쌰 🎶

Tao invites Van Binh to his first Korean baseball game, where they can enjoy the lively chants, wave their light sticks, and savour special baseball stadium food all at once!

LEARNING OBJECTIVES

- Describe personalities
- Provide a personal reason as the cause of an action
- Ask and answer to questions related to personal information
- Use vocabulary related to sports events and fandom
- Understand the main features of Korean baseball culture

GRAMMAR FOCUS

- -(으)니까(이유)
- -고 있다

KEY GRAMMAR AND EXPRESSIONS

1. -(으)니까(이유)

• **MEANING AND USAGE**

-(으)니까 is attached to the base of action and descriptive verbs to connect two sentences indicating that the first sentence provides the reason or basis for the second. It expresses causality, similar to -아/어서 (Unit 5). Despite sharing a similar meaning, the main differences are:

① -(으)니까 can be used when a request or command is expressed in the second sentence, whereas -아/어서 cannot be used in such cases.
② -(으)니까 expresses a subjective reason, while -아/어서 is used for objective, natural cause-effect relationships.
③ -(으)니까 can be attached to the past tense base (such as in -았/었으니까), while -아/어서 cannot.

• **STRUCTURE**

-으니까 is attached to verb bases ending with a consonant, while -니까 is attached to verb bases ending with a vowel.

타다 ➡ 타 + 니까 ➡ 타니까
맛있다 ➡ 맛있 + 으니까 ➡ 맛있으니까
예약하다 ➡ 예약하 + 니까 ➡ 예약하니까

• **EXAMPLES**

야구 티켓이 싸니까 자주 야구장에 가요.
➡ I often head to the baseball stadium because baseball tickets are affordable.

야구장에서 다 같이 응원하니까 정말 즐거웠어요.
➡ It was really enjoyable to cheer together at the baseball stadium.

한국 야구장은 밖에서 음식을 사서 들어갈 수 있으니까 좋아요.
➡ I enjoy Korean baseball stadium because you can buy and bring in food from outside.

타오: 날씨가 안 좋으니까 약속을 취소할까요?
The weather isn't good, so should we cancel the appointment?

반빈: 그래요!
Let's do that.

2. -고 있다

동료: 우미드, 주말에 뭐 할 거예요?
Umid, what are you up to this weekend?

우미드: 집에서 야구 보려고 해요.
I'm going to stay home and watch baseball.

동료: 경기장에는 안 가세요?
You're not going to the stadium?

우미드: 한국 핸드폰 번호가 없으니까 야구장 티켓을 예약할 수 없어요.
I don't have a Korean mobile number, so I can't book tickets to the stadium.

동료: 아… 수원 야구팀 앱에서는 이메일로 가입할 수 있어요. 티켓을 해외 카드로 살 수 있을 거예요.
Oh... You can sign up with your email on the Suwon Baseball Team app, and you can use an international credit card.

가브리엘: 약속 시간에 늦을까요?
Will we be late for the appointment?

하루: 지금 택시 탔으니까 괜찮을 거예요.
We just got a taxi now, so we should be fine.

• MEANING AND USAGE

-고 있다 is attached to the base of action verbs to indicate a continuing action. It functions similarly to the English present continuous form (be + V~ing). However, in Korean, -고 있다 can sometimes be used with verbs where English would not typically use the be + V~ing form-for example, 알고 있다 ("I know"). On the other hand, it cannot be used with verbs that describe actions completed in an instant, such as 도착하다 ("to arrive").

• STRUCTURE

-고 있다 is attached to verbs bases ending both in vowels and consonants.

자다 ➡ 자 + 고 있다 ➡ 자고 있어요
먹다 ➡ 먹 + 고 있다 ➡ 먹고 있어요
일하다 ➡ 일하 + 고 있다 ➡ 일하고 있어요

• **EXAMPLES**

저는 작년부터 한국에 살고 있어요.
➡ I've been living in Korea since last year.

주중에는 출근하기 전에 5km 정도 뛰고 있고 주말에는 10km 정도 뛰고 있습니다.
➡ During the week, I run about 5 kilometres before going to work, and on weekends I run about 10 kilometres.

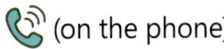 (on the phone)

가브리엘 지금 뭐 해?
What are you doing now?

소피아 게스트하우스에서 점심 먹고 있어.
I'm having lunch at the guest house.

 (on the phone)

사랑 지금 어디야
Where are you now?

하루 아, 지금 가고 있어. 거의 다 왔으니까 5분만 기다려줘.
Oh, I'm on my way, I'm almost there, give me five minutes.

샘 소피아, 왜 이렇게 늦게까지 안 자고 있어?
Sophia, why are you staying up so late?

소피아 요즘 고민이 많아서 잠이 잘 안 와.
I've been having a lot of trouble sleeping lately.

사랑 그 노래를 어떻게 알고 있어요? 아주 오래된 노래인데…
How do you know that song? It's a very old song.

파티마 저는 요즘 옛날 한국 노래도 많이 듣고 있어요.
I've been listening to a lot of old Korean songs lately.

대화 DIALOGUE

Tao is suggesting that Van Binh and he go watch a baseball game together.

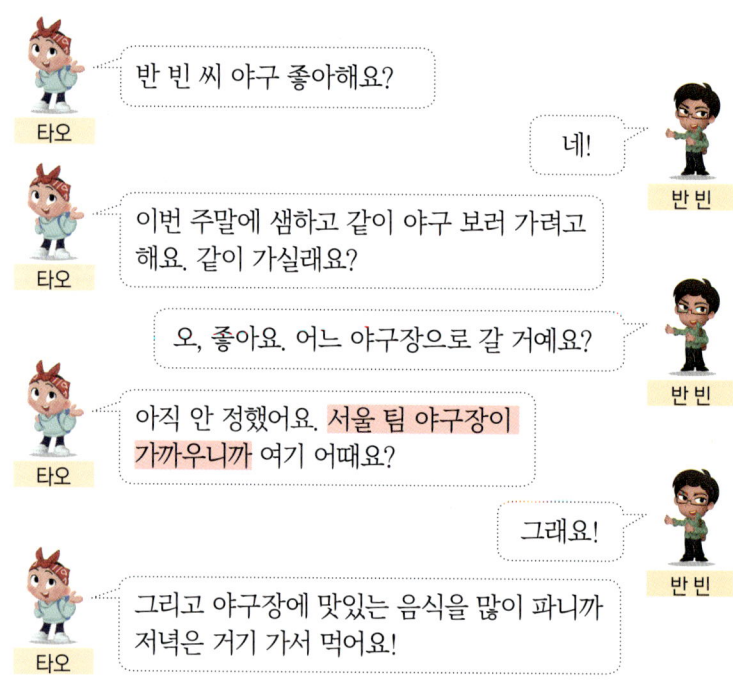

타오: 반 빈 씨 야구 좋아해요?
반 빈: 네!
타오: 이번 주말에 샘하고 같이 야구 보러 가려고 해요. 같이 가실래요?
반 빈: 오, 좋아요. 어느 야구장으로 갈 거예요?
타오: 아직 안 정했어요. 서울 팀 야구장이 가까우니까 여기 어때요?
반 빈: 그래요!
타오: 그리고 야구장에 맛있는 음식을 많이 파니까 저녁은 거기 가서 먹어요!

🗨️ **Role-play the dialogue by substituting the colour-coded words or phrases with the prompts below.**

서울 팀 야구장 - 가깝다

광주 팀 야구장 - 인기가 많다

대전 팀 야구장 - 팬 서비스가 좋다

부산 팀 야구장 - 응원이 더 신나다

Pre-reading Activity

Do you enjoy playing sports or watching them? If you prefer watching, have you ever seen a baseball game? What do you think you might find at a Korean baseball stadium?

Reading Activity

A baseball blogger conducted an interview with a Korean baseball fan. What does the fan enjoy most while watching a baseball game?

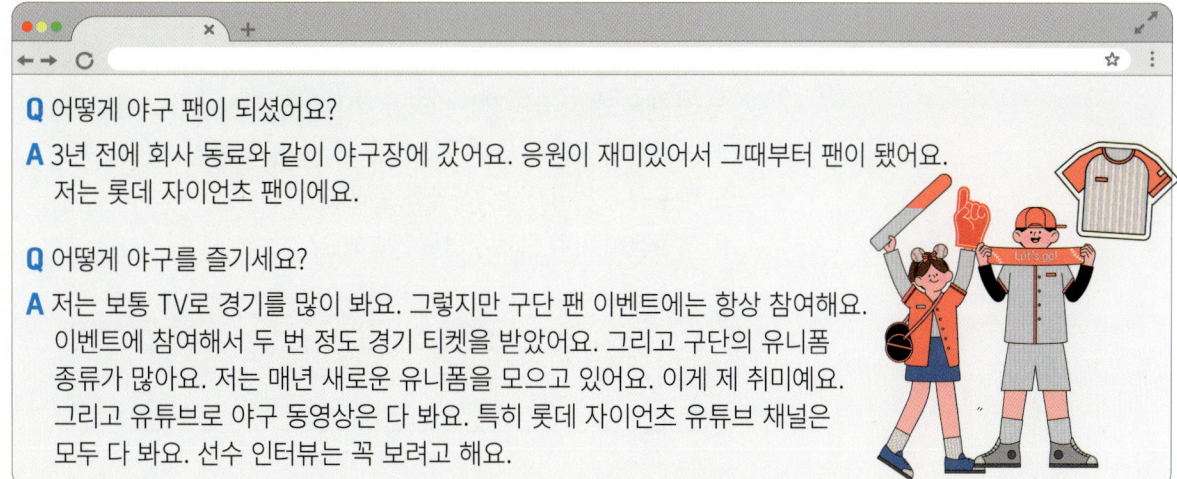

Q 어떻게 야구 팬이 되셨어요?
A 3년 전에 회사 동료와 같이 야구장에 갔어요. 응원이 재미있어서 그때부터 팬이 됐어요. 저는 롯데 자이언츠 팬이에요.

Q 어떻게 야구를 즐기세요?
A 저는 보통 TV로 경기를 많이 봐요. 그렇지만 구단 팬 이벤트에는 항상 참여해요. 이벤트에 참여해서 두 번 정도 경기 티켓을 받았어요. 그리고 구단의 유니폼 종류가 많아요. 저는 매년 새로운 유니폼을 모으고 있어요. 이게 제 취미예요. 그리고 유튜브로 야구 동영상은 다 봐요. 특히 롯데 자이언츠 유튜브 채널은 모두 다 봐요. 선수 인터뷰는 꼭 보려고 해요.

READING

Q 온라인과 오프라인 굿즈샵에서 뭘 구매했어요?
A 유니폼하고 모자, 그리고 머리띠를 샀어요.

Q 경기를 야구장에 가서 직접 보면 뭐가 좋아요?
A 응원과 야구장 음식이요. 보통 팬들이 야구단 유니폼을 입고 모자를 써요. 그리고 다 같이 춤을 추고 응원가를 불러요. 분위기가 노래방 같아요. 꼭 다 같이 응원가를 함께 불러 보세요. 그럼 야구장의 분위기를 더 잘 즐길 수 있어요. 저도 팀을 응원하려고 야구장에 가기 전에 응원가를 연습해요. 그리고 야구장에서 맛있는 음식을 즐길 수 있어요. 야구장 안에서는 치킨, 새우 튀김, 피자를 팔아요. 삼겹살 도시락 세트도 있어요. 그리고 야구장 밖에서는 보통 떡볶이, 만두를 팔아요. 야구장 음식은 정말 다양하고 맛있어요!

Q 경기를 야구장에 가서 직접 보면 뭐가 불편해요?
A 이 구단 야구장이 조금 오래됐어요. 그래서 자리가 조금 좁아요. 그리고 경기가 끝난 후에 많은 사람들이 한번에 나가니까 교통이 복잡하고 지하철을 많이 기다려야 해요. 그래서 저는 보통 8회쯤 경기가 끝나기 전에 집에 가요.

A. Check off the statement if it is correct.

1. 팬 이벤트에 참여해요. 그러면 경기 티켓을 받을 수 있어요. ☐
2. 이 팬은 TV보다 경기장에서 경기를 많이 봐요. ☐
3. 굿즈 샵에서는 유니폼, 목도리, 장갑을 살 수 있어요. ☐
4. 야구장에서 팬들은 조용히 경기를 봐요. ☐
5. 야구장에서 구단의 응원가를 불러요. 그럼 야구장 분위기를 잘 즐길 수 있어요. ☐
6. 야구장 밖에서는 삼겹살 도시락 세트와 만두를 살 수 있어요. ☐

B. Answer the question and then ask your partner.

1. 이 사람은 언제 롯데 자이언츠 팬이 됐어요?
2. 이 사람의 야구 취미는 뭐예요?
3. 이 팬은 왜 자주 경기를 보러 못 가요? (두 가지)
4. 야구장에 직접 가서 야구를 봐요. 그럼 뭐가 좋아요? (두 가지)
5. 야구장 분위기가 어디하고 비슷해요?
6. 야구장에 가기 전에 무엇을 연습해요?

C. 야구장에 가서 야구를 본 후에 집에 갈 때 이 사람은 뭐가 불편해요? 그래서 어떻게 해요?

1) _____

2) _____

READING

After-reading Activity

You are at a baseball game. Before the start of the game, you go to the merchandise and food section of the stadium to buy some items. Look at the images below and explain what you want to buy. Make sure to explain the reason too!

구단 매장에서:

- 유니폼
- 야구 모자
- 야구 점퍼
- 머리띠

야구장 매점에서:

- 떡볶이와 어묵
- 핫도그와 회오리 감자
- 치킨과 소떡소떡
- 피자
- 삼겹살 도시락

_____
_____
_____
_____
_____
_____
_____
_____

Pre-listening Activity

Imagine being a sports news reporter. Consider the topics you may interview the athletes or celebrities on. Think about what you would ask and collaborate with your partner to create a list of questions for your interview.

☑ 성격: e.g., 영수 씨는 어떤 사람이에요?
☑ 음식: _____
☑ 여행 : _____
☑ 취미: _____
☑ ? : _____
☑ ? : _____

Listening Activity

A baseball player, Yeongsoo Jeong, participates in a casual Q&A session on his team's YouTube channel. What topics are discussed in the interview?

A. Listen to the audio file and then select any correct statement.

1. 정영수 선수 생일은 10월 12일이에요.
2. 정영수 선수의 성격은 긍정적이고 쉽게 친구를 사귀어요.
3. 정영수 선수의 보물 1호는 가족이에요.
4. 정영수 선수는 프로필 사진을 다른 나라에 가서 찍었어요.
5. 정영수 선수는 휴일에 보통 집에서 10시간 잠을 자요.

B. Ask and answer the following questions with your partners.

1. 정영수 선수는 요즘 무슨 앱을 자주 써요?
2. 정영수 선수는 어떤 여행을 기억하고 있어요? 어디로 여행 가고 싶어해요? 왜 그 곳에 가고 싶어해요?
3. 정영수 선수는 어떤 음식을 매일 먹을 수 있어요?
4. 정영수 선수는 어떤 다른 스포츠를 좋아해요? 그리고 언제 이 스포츠를 해요?
5. 정영수 선수는 어느 야구팀을 제일 좋아해요? 왜 야구 선수가 되고 싶어했어요?
6. 정영수 선수는 팬들에게 무엇을 말했어요?

 활동 ACTIVITY

Interview your partner by asking questions about their basic information and preferences. Below are some suggested keywords. Remember to use -(으)니까 and -고 있다.

- [x] 이름
- [x] 생년월일
- [x] 성격(장점과 단점)
- [x] 보물 1호
- [x] 프로필 사진
- [x] 앱
- [x] 매일 먹는 음식
- [x] 여행
- [x] 휴일
- [x] 스포츠
- [x] 응원팀

"으쌰라 으쌰 ♪♪"

**Korea's Love for Sports:
Playing vs. Watching**

Koreans have a deep love for both playing and watching sports. Hiking is a particularly popular activity, with the country's landscape being 70% mountainous and offering trails for all levels of hikers.

It's common to see people of all ages, decked out in professional hiking gear, enjoying breathtaking views and the camaraderie of hiking groups. On the other hand, baseball and soccer dominate as the most-watched sports.

Baseball games, in particular, are more than just matches-they're vibrant social events. Fans come together for cheering songs, coordinated chants, and even themed food, creating an atmosphere that's uniquely Korean and full of energy.

Korean Baseball Cheering Song Source (QR code) from: [#again_playlist] 으쌰라 으쌰 으쌰라 으쌰♬✨ KBO 야구 응원가👊 모음.zip | KBS 방송

K-MEDIA CORNER

Baseball scenes in K-dramas often reflect Korean culture and community spirit. *Hot Stove League* (스토브리그) focuses on the challenges of managing a struggling baseball team, highlighting the passion and dedication behind the sport. In *Twenty-Five Twenty-One* (스물다섯 스물하나), baseball brings characters together, showing how the sport is a fun way to relax and bond.

Doctor Prisoner (닥터 프리즈너) uses baseball to create personal connections, even in tough settings like a prison. These dramas show how baseball goes beyond the game, creating connections and moments of growth. Alongside the dramas, there are variety shows featuring retired baseball players and amateurs who continue their baseball journey with passion.

 How do K-dramas use baseball to show teamwork and connection between characters?

 What can we learn about Korean culture from the way baseball is portrayed in these dramas and variety shows?

[이미지 출처: 네이버/유튜브]

실제 표현
Real Expressions

[50문 50답 50 Questions and Answers]

- 현재 즐겨 쓰는 앱 3개는?
→ Which three apps do you use most frequently?

- 매일 먹어도 질리지 않는 음식은?
→ What food could you eat daily without growing bored?

- 가장 기억에 남는 여행은?
→ What has been your most unforgettable trip?

- 쉬는 날 꼭 하는 일은?
→ What activities do you consistently engage in during your days off?

- 야구를 제외하고 좋아하는 스포츠는?
→ Besides baseball, which sports do you enjoy?

☑ Now I know these!
Mark off what you learnt (grammar, vocabulary, usage)

- 서울 팀 야구장이 가까우니까 여기로 갈까요? ☑
- 매년 새로운 유니폼을 모으고 있어요. ☐
- 응원가를 불러요. ☐
- 쇼핑 앱 ☐
- 저는 긍정적인 사람이에요. ☐
- 달리기 ☐

10과

바당밭과 숨비소리

The friends explore the stunning Jeju Island, enjoy its beaches, and meet a haenyeo diver, a guardian of nature, while learning about the haenyeo's inspiring history.

LEARNING OBJECTIVES

- Express intention
- Express negation
- Understand the visual representation of simple statistical data
- Use vocabulary related to sustainable work activities
- Understand the work of female divers in a contemporary world

GRAMMAR FOCUS

- –지 않다
- –지 못하다
- –(으)려고 + 동사

KEY GRAMMAR AND EXPRESSIONS

1. –지 않다

• MEANING AND USAGE

-지 않다 is attached to the base of action and descriptive verbs to indicate a negation. It is the long version of the negative form 안 (see volume 1, Unit 7). Depending on the context, the usage of -지 않다/안 with some action verbs can indicate that something has not been done due to the subject's intention or will. 안 is placed in front of verbs and -지 않다 is attached to the base of verbs. Both have the same meaning, although -지 않다 is preferred in formal writing.

• STRUCTURE

-지 않다 is attached to verb bases ending in both vowels and consonants.

타다 → 타 + 지 않아요 → 타지 않아요
먹다 → 먹 + 지 않아요 → 먹지 않아요
수영하다 → 수영하 + 지 않아요 → 수영하지 않아요

• EXAMPLES

겨울입니다. 그런데 아직 춥지 않습니다.
→ It's winter, but it isn't cold yet.

옛날에는 해녀가 많았지만 요즘은 많지 않습니다.
→ Once upon a time, there were many haenyeo female divers, but these days, not as many.

해녀 일은 쉽지 않습니다.
→ A haenyeo's work is not easy.

해녀들은 어린 해산물은 잡지 않습니다.
The haenyeo don't catch young seafood.

저는 친구와 같이 바다에 갔어요. 저는 바다에서 수영을 하고 싶었어요. 그런데 친구는 수영하고 싶어하지 않았어요.
→ I went to the sea with my friend. I wanted to swim, but my friend didn't want to.

2. –지 못하다

• MEANING AND USAGE

-지 못하다 is attached to the base of action verbs to indicate a negative meaning when actions happen because of something beyond the subject's will. It is the long version of the negative form 못 (see volume 1, Unit 8). Although the long and the short version have the same meaning, the long version is preferred in formal writing.

• STRUCTURE

-지 못하다 is attached to verb bases ending in both vowels and consonants.

자다 ➡ 자 + 지 못해요 ➡ 자지 못해요
먹다 ➡ 먹 + 지 못해요 ➡ 먹지 못해요
수영하다 ➡ 수영하 + 지 못해요 ➡ 수영하지 못해요

• EXAMPLES

우미드 씨는 아침에 늦잠을 잤어요. 그래서 회사에 빨리 가야 했어요. 세수도 하지 못하고 이도 닦지 못 했어요.
➡ Umid overslept in the morning, so he had to rush to work. He didn't wash his face or brush his teeth.

사랑: 왜 등산하러 안 갔어요?
Why didn't you go hiking?

하루: 어제 다리를 다쳐서 등산하러 가지 못했어요.
I hurt my leg yesterday, so I couldn't go hiking.

기자: 성격이 어떠세요?
What is your personality like?

야구 선수: 저는 처음에 사람들을 쉽게 사귀지 못해요.
I don't easily get along with people at first

3. -(으)려고 + 동사

• MEANING AND USAGE

As seen in Unit 6, -(으)려고 is used to indicate an intention or goal. When -(으)려고 is attached to the verb in the first sentence, the second sentence expresses the action done in order to achieve that goal. (으)려고 functions similiarly to "in order to," in English. For this reason, the subject of the first sentence must be the same as the second sentence.

• STRUCTURE

-으려고 is attached to verb bases ending with a consonant, while -려고 is attached to verb bases ending with a vowel

자다 ➡ 자 + 려고 ➡ 자려고
먹다 ➡ 먹 + 으려고 ➡ 먹으려고
수영하다 ➡ 수영하 + 려고 ➡ 수영하려고

• EXAMPLES

크리스마스 때 멜버른에 가려고 돈을 모으고 있어요.
➡ I'm saving money to go to Melbourne for Christmas.

해녀들은 바다를 지키려고 해산물을 손으로 잡아요.
➡ Haenyeo catch seafood with their hands to help protect the ocean.

사랑: 여보세요? 숨비소리 게스트하우스입니다.
Hello, this is Sumbisori Guest House.

손님: 아, 네. 오늘 체크인하려고 전화드렸습니다.
Oh, I'm calling to check in today.

소피아: 마두카 씨, 떡볶이를 왜 이렇게 많이 샀어요?
Maduka, why did you buy so much tteokbokki?

마두카: 게스트하우스 친구하고 다 같이 먹으려고 많이 샀어요.
I bought a lot of tteokbokki to share with my friends at the guest house.

소피아: 우와, 고마워요! 마두카 씨!
Wow, thank you, Maduka.

사랑: 캐롤라인 씨, 뭐 하세요?
Caroline, what are you doing?

캐롤라인: 한국 소설을 읽으려고 한국어를 배우고 있어요.
I'm learning Korean so I can read Korean novels.

대화 DIALOGUE

Sarang and Caroline went down to the shore to say hello to Sarang's grandmother, Seondeok, who works as a haenyeo.

선덕 할머니: 바다까지 왜 나왔어? 집에서 기다리지?

사랑: 캐롤라인 씨가 해녀에 관심이 많아서 할머니 보러 같이 왔어요.

캐롤라인: 안녕하세요?

선덕 할머니: 그래요. 잘 왔어요.

캐롤라인: 어… 할머니, 해녀 일이 힘들지 않으세요?

선덕 할머니: 아니요. 즐거워요.

Role-play the dialogue by substituting the colour-coded words or phrases with the prompts below.

해녀 일이 힘들다 – 아니요. 즐거워요.

춥다 – 네. 안 추워요.

어린 해산물을 잡다 – 네. 안 잡아요.

혼자 일하다 – 네. 혼자 일 안 해요.

해산물을 한꺼번에 많이 잡다 – 네. 많이 안 잡아요.

 **Pre-reading Activity**

Take a look at the bar graph below, which shows the population of Jeju Island. What units are used to count the people? What is the total number of people in Jeju? What information can you read from the graph?

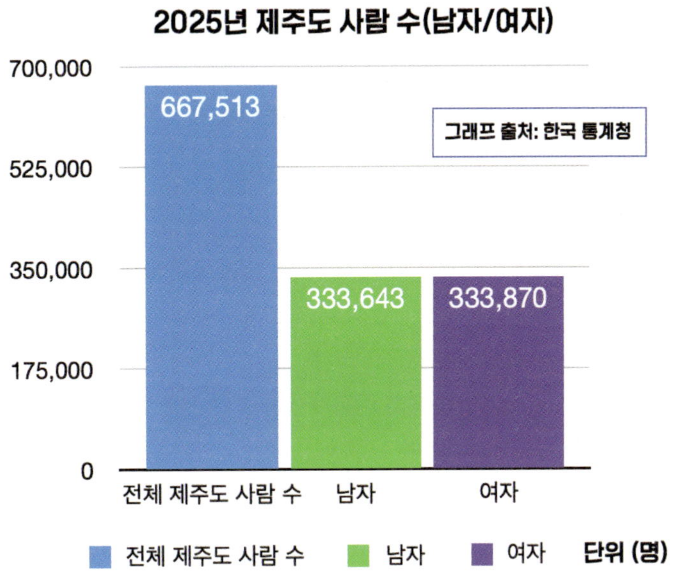

2025년 제주도 사람 수(남자/여자)

전체 제주도 사람 수	667,513
남자	333,643
여자	333,870

그래프 출처: 한국 통계청

단위 (명)

📖 **Quick check-in: Select the correct statement from the graph above.**

1. 제주도에는 60만 명 이상의 사람이 살고 있어요. ☐
2. 이 그래프의 단위는 '명'이에요. ☐
3. 여자가 남자보다 많지 않아요. ☐

_____

_____

_____

_____

READING

 **Reading Activity**

Review graph 1 and chart 1, then discuss the topic with your partner. What does this refer to?

_____

_____

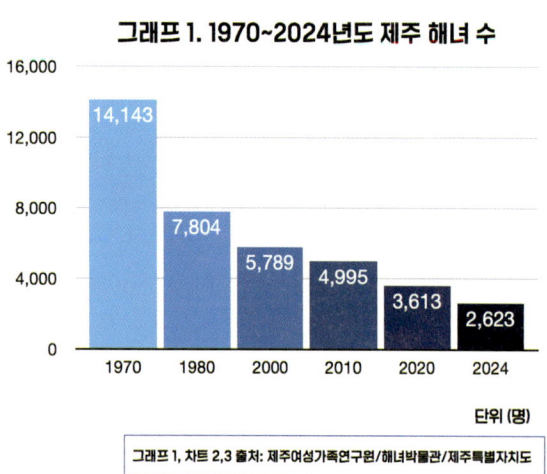

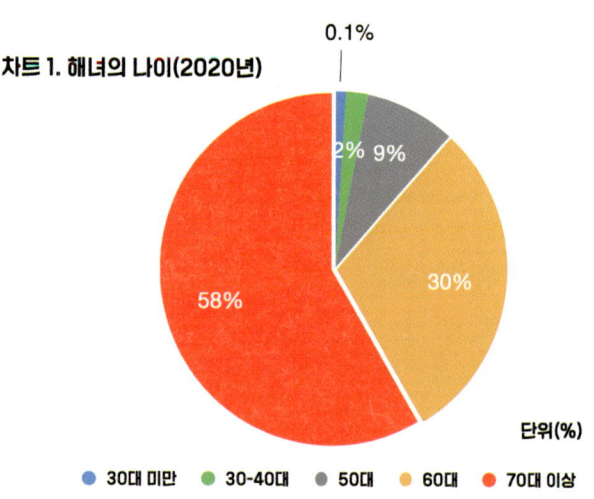

A. Check off the statement if it is correct.

1. 그래프 1과 차트 1은 해녀들에 대해 이야기하고 있어요. ☐
2. 1970년부터 지금까지 사람들이 해녀 일을 점점 더 많이 해요. ☐
3. 2000년도의 해녀 수는 4,995명이었어요. ☐
4. 60대 이상의 해녀들은 88%예요. ☐
5. 차트 1에서 30~40대 해녀들은 50대 해녀 보다 많지 않아요. ☐

B. Answer the question and then ask your partner.

1. 그래프 1과 차트 1은 무엇에 대해 이야기 하고 있어요?
2. 옛날과 지금 모두 해녀 수가 많아요?
3. 1970년보다 2024년도에 해녀는 얼마나 더 적어요?
4. 30대 미만 해녀들이 많아요?
5. 앞으로 해녀 직업은 어떻게 될까요?

READING

 **After-reading Activity**

Look at the chart below regarding haenyeo in their thirties and forties. Discuss the number with your partner and then respond to the following question.

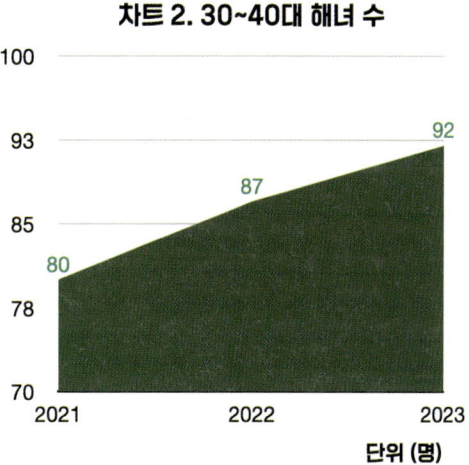

▶ 옛날에는 해녀가 많았어요. 지금은 2,623명 밖에 없어요. 그런데 2021년부터 2023년까지 30~40대 해녀들이 점점 더 많이 생겼어요. 여러분은 이것에 대해 어떻게 생각하세요?

듣기 LISTENING

Pre-listening Activity

Create a mini-dialogue using the given words and expressions as shown in the example.

E.g. A: 한국에서 최초의 여성 직업은 뭐예요?
      B: 글쎄요…잘 모르겠어요.

- ☑ 최초: the first
- ☑ 여성: female
- ☑ 해산물: seafood
- ☑ 잡다: to catch/hold/take
- ☑ 자연을 지키다: to protect nature
- ☑ 도와주다: to help someone

_____
_____
_____
_____
_____

Listening Activity

Caroline visits the Haenyeo Museum and participates in the museum's lecture series. What is the primary topic of the lecture?

A. Listen to the audio file and then select any correct statement.

1. 해녀는 우리 나라 최초의 여성 직업이 아니에요. ☐
2. 해녀 직업은 아주 오래 되었어요. ☐
3. 해녀들은 일을 해서 마을 사람들만 도와줬어요. ☐
4. 7~8살 때부터 조금 먼 바다에서 해녀 일을 배워요. ☐
5. 해녀 일은 혼자서 하지 못해요. ☐

B. Ask and answer the following questions with your partners.

1. 보통 해산물을 어떻게 잡아요?
2. 해녀들은 자연을 지키고 싶어해요. 그래서 어떻게 일을 해요?
3. 해녀 일은 왜 혼자서 하지 못해요?

C. 해녀들은 일은 한 후에 돈도 함께 나눴어요. 이렇게 해서 누구를 도와줬어요?

_____

활동 ACTIVITY

Review the lecture series and then discuss the haenyeo with your partner, using insights from the audio file featuring -지 않다/-지 못하다, as well as the images and vocabulary provided below.

- 해산물
- 손으로 잡다
- 나이가 적다
- 자연을 지키다
- 최초
- 바닷가
- 돈을 나누다

_____
_____
_____
_____
_____
_____

"바당밭과 숨비소리"

Culture Corner:
Haenyeo - Guardians of Sustainable Living

Jeju's haenyeo, or "sea women," embody a unique combination of resilience, community, and sustainability. Their diving tradition, with roots as far back as the 5th century, initially began as a male profession. However, by the 18th century, it became predominantly female, shaped by historical and environmental factors, such as men's involvement in wars and the natural advantages women possess for diving in cold waters.

Haenyeo free-dive without oxygen tanks, harvesting seafood like abalone, seaweed, and shellfish. This work is not only physically demanding but deeply tied to sustainability. Haenyeo are mindful of harvesting practices, taking only what the sea can replenish. During the Joseon dynasty, haenyeo were required to offer their catches as tribute, reflecting their significance in Korea's cultural and economic history.

Recognized by UNESCO in 2016, haenyeo culture is more than a profession; it represents an eco-conscious lifestyle. The haenyeo's methods have evolved, but their core values of community and respect for nature remain steadfast. Modern haenyeo continue to inspire as pioneers of sustainable coexistence with the natural world.

K-MEDIA CORNER

Jeju Island's breathtaking scenery and rich cultural heritage make it a popular setting in K-dramas, showcasing the unique charm of Korea's southern island. *Our Blues* (우리들의 블루스) captures the everyday lives of Jeju's residents, including the resilient haenyeo (female divers), whose stories reflect the island's deep connection to the sea.

Warm and Cozy (맨도롱 또똣) highlights the romance and challenges of life on Jeju, blending beautiful coastal views with the ups and downs of running a restaurant by the sea. *Tamra, The Island* (탐나는도다) transports viewers to historical Jeju, focusing on the island's distinct traditions and the lives of its people, including haenyeo and traders.

These dramas celebrate Jeju's natural beauty, its vibrant community, and the inspiring spirit of those who call the island home, much like Sarang and her friends' memorable visit in *Annyeong? Korean!*

 How do dramas like *Our Blues*, and *Warm and Cozy* portray the unique lifestyle and cultural heritage of Jeju Island's residents?

 What role does the setting of Jeju Island play in shaping the stories and characters in K-dramas, and how does it enhance the narrative?

[이미지 출처: 네이버/유튜브]

실제 표현
Real Expressions

- 첫 번째 차트는 1970년대부터 2020년대까지의 해녀 인구수에 대해 이야기하고 있습니다.
→ The first chart illustrates the number of female divers from the 1970s to the 2020s.

- 두 번째 차트에서는 연령별 해녀 인구를 비교했습니다. 70대 이상의 해녀가 59%로 전체 중에서 제일 많습니다. 60세 이상을 포함한 해녀 인구수는 전체의 89%가 됩니다. 30대 이하 해녀는 0.1%로 거의 없습니다.
→ The second chart compares the number of female divers by age, revealing that those aged 70 and above account for 59% of the total. Meanwhile, female divers aged 60 and over represent 89% of the total.

- 세 번째 차트는 30대에서 40대까지의 해녀 인구수입니다. 전체 해녀 수는 계속 줄고 있지만 30~40대 해녀 수는 2021년부터 2023년까지 증가했습니다.
→ There are almost no female divers aged 30 and below, making up only 0.1%. The third chart depicts the number of female divers aged 30 to 40. Although the total number of female divers has been decreasing, the number of female divers aged 30 to 40 has increased from 2021 to 2023.

☑ Now I know these!
Mark off what you learnt (grammar, vocabulary, usage)

- 해녀 일이 힘들지 않으세요? ☑
- 해녀는 우리 나라 최초의 여성 직업이에요. ☐
- 자연을 지켜야 해요. ☐
- 해녀 일은 혼자서 하지 못합니다. ☐
- 해녀들은 바다를 지키려고 해산물을 손으로 잡아요. ☐

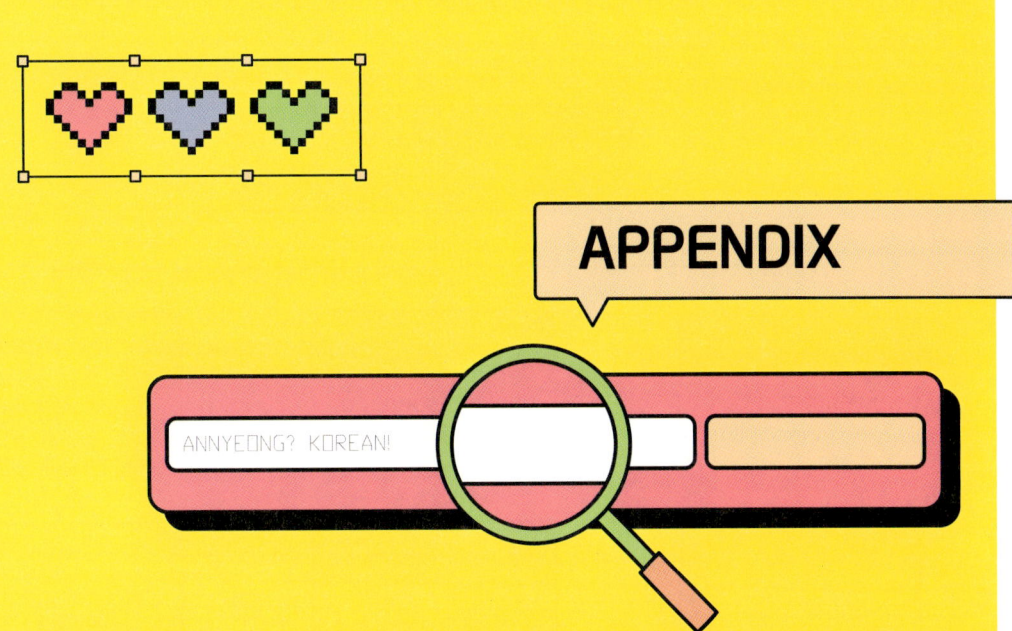

Appendix 01: Irregular Conjugations

Many Korean verbal suffixes are attached to action and descriptive verbs depending on the shape of the verb base. Below is a summary of how the verbal suffixes in *Annyeong? Korean!* volumes 1 and 2 are attached to verb bases.

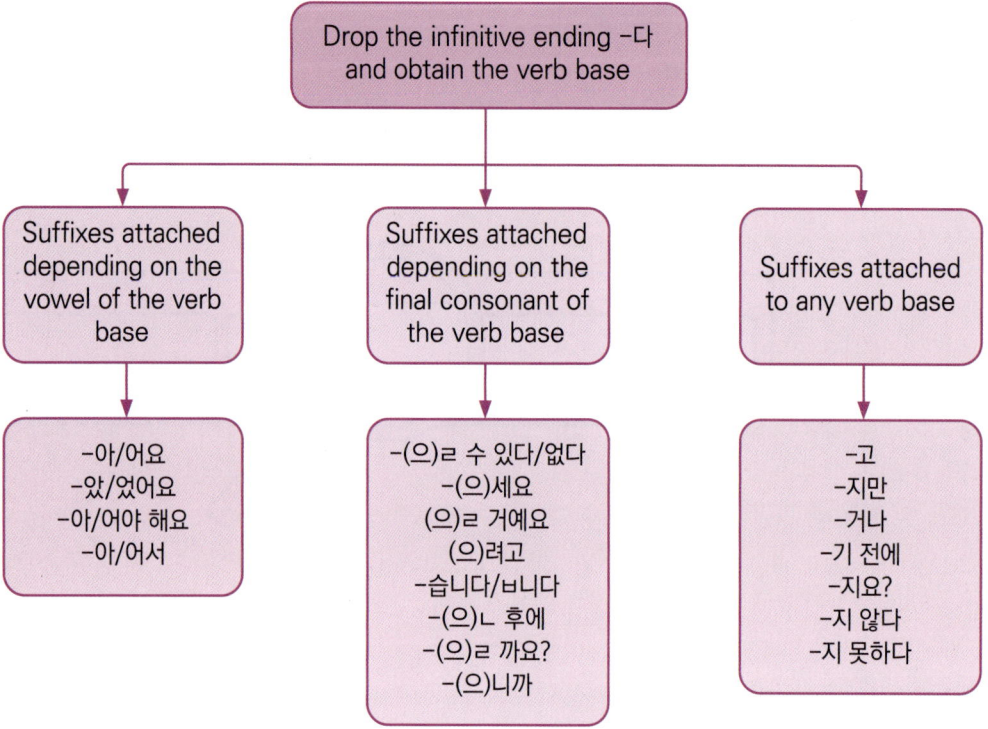

Some verbs, depending on the last vowel or consonant of their base, may modify the base itself before attaching certain suffixes, in many cases depending on whether the suffix begin with a consonant or a vowel. You can use the summary below to see which kind of verbs change the shape of the base.

✏ Verb base ending with ㄷ

ㄷ changes into ㄹ in front of suffixes beginning with vowels.

듣다 + 어요 ➡ 들 + 어요 ➡ 들어요

듣다 + 을 거예요 ➡ 들 + 을 거예요 ➡ 들을 거예요

Caution: not all verbs which base ends in ㄷ are irregular (e.g., 받다 ➡ 받아요, 받을 거예요)

✏️ Verb base ending with ㅡ

ㅡ is dropped in front of suffixes beginning with -아/어.

바쁘다 + 아요 ➡ 바ㅃ + 아요 ➡ 바빠요

쓰다 + 어요 ➡ ㅆ + 어요 ➡ 써요

✏️ Verb base ending with ㄹ

ㄹ is dropped in front of suffixes beginning with ㄴ, ㅂ, ㅅ, 으.

살다 + ㅂ니다 ➡ 사 + ㅂ니다 ➡ 삽니다

만들다 + (으)세요 ➡ 만드 + 세요 ➡ 만드세요

✏️ Verb base ending with 르

ㅡ is dropped and ㄹ is doubled in front of suffixes beginning with -아/어.

모르다 + 아요 ➡ 몰ㄹ + 아요 ➡ 몰라요

빠르다 + 아여 ➡ 빨ㄹ + 아요 ➡ 빨라요

✏️ Verb base ending with ㅂ

ㅂ becomes 우 in front of suffixes beginning with vowels.

춥다 + 어요 ➡ 추우 + 어요 ➡ 추워요

맵다 + 어서 ➡ 매우 + 어서 ➡ 매워서

덥다 + (으)ㄹ 수 있어요 ➡ 더우 + ㄹ 수 있어요 ➡ 더울 수 있어요

Caution: only descriptive verbs changes as illustrated, processive verbs which base ends with ㅂ retains ㅂ (e.g., 입다 ➡ 입어요; 입어서)

✏️ Verb base ending with ㅅ

ㅅ in front of suffixes beginning with vowels.

낫다 + 아요 ➡ 나 + 아요 ➡ 나아요

낫다 + (으)ㄹ 거예요 ➡ 나을 거예요

Appendix 02: 존댓말 and 반말

The indication of a formal or an informal polite speech level and of an intimate speech level depends mostly on the use of verbal endings and pronouns. In the case of verbal endings, most often only 요 is dropped, but there can be other changes as illustrated in the tables below.

✏ Plain statements

Informal polite speech level	Intimate speech level
어제 야구장에 갔어요.	어제 야구장에 갔어.
오늘 백화점에 사람이 많아요.	오늘 백화점에 사람이 많아.
내일 눈이 올 거예요.	내일 눈이 올 거야.
타오 씨가 바쁜 것 같아요.	타오 씨가 바쁜 것 같아.
제 이름은 캐롤라인이에요.	내 이름은 캐롤라인이야.

✏ Questions

Informal polite speech level	Intimate speech level
어제 강릉에 잘 갔다 오셨어요?	어제 강릉에 잘 갔다 왔어?
이 음식 이름이 뭐예요?	이 음식 이름이 뭐야?

✏ Imperative

Informal polite speech level	Intimate speech level
이따 전화하세요.	이따 전화해.
술을 많이 드시지 마세요.	술을 많이 마시지 마.

📝 Suggestions and requests

Informal polite speech level	Intimate speech level
같이 기차 여행을 갈까요?	같이 기차 여행을 갈까?
같이 가요!	같이 가자!

📝 Plain statements

Informal polite speech level	Intimate speech level
저	나
제가	내가
제거	내거
(상대방)	너
(상대방) + 가	네가
(상대방) + 것	네거
소피아 씨	소피아야
네	응
아니요	아니야
안녕하세요	안녕
안녕히 계세요	잘 있어
안녕히 가세요	잘 가

Appendix 03 Word list (Korean to English, by unit)

1과

1과	가방	bag
1과	갓	traditional Korean hat
1과	개인	individual/personal
1과	건축	architecture
1과	검색하다	search, to
1과	고맙다	thankful, be
1과	공지 사항	announcement/notice
1과	공짜	free of charge
1과	관람	viewing/watching (an exhibition)
1과	그래서	then
1과	그리고	and
1과	기대하다	expect, to
1과	꽃신	traditional decorated Korean shoes
1과	남다	left, to be
1과	남색	navy
1과	내국인	domestic person
1과	내다	pay, to
1과	노란색	yellow
1과	늦다	late, to be
1과	다르다	different, to be
1과	단체	group
1과	대여	rental
1과	돈	money
1과	두루마기	traditional Korean overcoat
1과	들어가다	enter, to
1과	뜻	meaning
1과	리뷰	review
1과	마음에 들다	satisfied/happy with something, to be
1과	마이크	microphone
1과	만나다	meet, to
1과	많다	many, to be
1과	말하다	speak/say, to
1과	맡기다	leave/deposit, to
1과	매일	every day
1과	먼저	first, in advance
1과	무료	free of charge
1과	바지	pants
1과	받다	receive, to
1과	보관함	storage cabinet
1과	보라색	purple
1과	비싸다	expensive, to be
1과	빨간색	red
1과	사람	people
1과	사진	photo
1과	스페인어	Spanish language
1과	시간	time
1과	시작하다	start, to
1과	신나다	excited, to be
1과	신다	wear (shoes), to
1과	쓰다	wear (hat/cap), to
1과	안내	information
1과	알다	know, to
1과	약속	appointment, promise
1과	언어	language
1과	영상	video
1과	영어	English language
1과	옷	dress/clothes
1과	외국인	foreign person
1과	요금	fee/charge
1과	유튜브	YouTube
1과	일찍	early
1과	입다	wear, to
1과	입장	admission
1과	저고리	traditional Korean jacket
1과	전통	tradition/traditional
1과	정말	really
1과	조금	a little
1과	주말	weekend
1과	주황색	orange
1과	지하철	subway
1과	찍다	take (a photo/a video), to
1과	착용	wear, to
1과	찾다	find/look for, to
1과	초록색	green
1과	치마	skirt
1과	큰일나다	serious, be (said of a situation)
1과	타다	take (a mean of transportation), to
1과	탈의실	change room
1과	파란색	blue
1과	파일	file (computer)
1과	프랑스어	French language
1과	하루	a day/one day
1과	하얀색	white
1과	한복	Korean traditional dress

2과

2과	가끔	sometimes
2과	가다	go, to
2과	괜찮다	okay/fine, to be
2과	국제특급	international express
2과	끝나다	finish, to
2과	나이	age

2과	높다	high/tall, be
2과	누구	who
2과	대리	assistant manager
2과	듣다	listen, to
2과	마시다	drink, to
2과	막히다	blocked/jammed, to be
2과	말실수	slip of the tongue
2과	먹다	eat, to
2과	모임	gathering
2과	문화	culture
2과	반말	informal speech
2과	밥	rice/meal
2과	보내다	send, to
2과	빌리다	borrow, to
2과	빠르다	quick/fast, to be
2과	사장님	boss
2과	산	mountain
2과	생활	life
2과	술	alcohol
2과	식사하다	have a meal, to
2과	신입 사원	new employee
2과	어렵다	difficult, to be
2과	우체국	post office
2과	웃다	laugh/smile, to
2과	원래	originally
2과	이해하다	understand, to
2과	일하다	work, to
2과	자세하다	detailed, to be
2과	잘하다	do well, to
2과	재미있다	interesting/fun, to be
2과	점심	lunch
2과	존댓말	formal language
2과	좋다	good, to be
2과	참석하다	attend, to
2과	처음	first/beginning
2과	추천하다	suggest, to
2과	축하하다	congratulate, to
2과	취직하다	get a job, to
2과	친절하다	kind, to be
2과	콜라	coke
2과	특히	especially/in particular
2과	편하다	comfortable, to be
2과	프로젝트	project
2과	한반도	Korean peninsula
2과	할머니	grandmother
2과	형	older brother
2과	호주	Australia
2과	환영하다	welcome, to
2과	환영회	welcome party
2과	회식	company dinner

3과

3과	가격	price
3과	가깝다	near, to be
3과	가운데	middle/centre
3과	갑자기	suddenly
3과	고글	goggles
3과	고르다	choose/select, to
3과	국가	country
3과	근처	nearby
3과	기차역	train station
3과	기차표	train ticket
3과	깨끗하다	clean, to be
3과	나중에	later
3과	넓다	wide/spacious, to be
3과	놀다	play/hang out, to
3과	닭강정	sweet fried chicken nuggets
3과	대표	representative
3과	마을 버스	trolley bus
3과	멈추다	stop, to
3과	모르다	not know, to
3과	모자	hat/cap
3과	미리	in advance
3과	베트남	Vietnam
3과	별로	not really (used with negative verbs)
3과	보이다	seen, to be
3과	부츠	boots
3과	비자	visa
3과	사고	accident
3과	사우나	sauna
3과	선택하다	choose/select, to
3과	셔틀버스	shuttle bus
3과	숙박 시설	accommodation
3과	스키	ski
3과	스키장	ski resort
3과	시키다	order, to
3과	신분증	ID card
3과	아주머니	ma'am
3과	안전	safety
3과	알리다	inform/let know, to
3과	야간	night time
3과	야구	baseball
3과	얼른	quickly
3과	여권	passport
3과	영화	film
3과	오전	morning
3과	오후	afternoon
3과	움직이다	move, to
3과	위험하다	dangerous, to be
3과	이따가	later (usually within the same day)
3과	이용 시간	operating hours
3과	장갑	gloves
3과	장비	equipment
3과	장소	place
3과	조심하다	careful, to be
3과	주의 사항	precautions

3과	준비 운동	warm-up exercise
3과	준비하다	prepare, to
3과	지금	now
3과	직원	employee
3과	참치	tuna
3과	축제	festival
3과	친구	friend
3과	케이크	cake
3과	택시	taxi
3과	평일	weekday
3과	포스터	poster
3과	헬멧	helmet
3과	혹시	perhaps
3과	횡단보도	zebra crossing

4과

4과	가수	singer
4과	가져 가다	take (something), to
4과	걷다	walk, to
4과	걸다	hang, to
4과	고등학생	high school student
4과	공부하다	study, to
4과	공연	show/performance
4과	굿즈 부스	merchandise booth
4과	그룹	group
4과	나오다	appear/come out, to
4과	내리다	get off, to
4과	노래	song
4과	다시	again
4과	대답	answer
4과	대중 가요	pop song
4과	돕다	help, to
4과	동영상	video
4과	말씀하다	speak, to (polite)
4과	매점	store
4과	미국	US
4과	반갑다	glad, to be
4과	밤	night
4과	방금	just now
4과	방송	broadcast
4과	배우	actor/actress
4과	버컬	vocal
4과	보물	treasure
4과	보통	usually
4과	사용하다	use, to
4과	새롭다	new, to be
4과	소개하다	introduce, to
4과	소속사	entertainment company, agency
4과	수업	class
4과	스피치	speech
4과	아이돌	idol
4과	아침	morning
4과	앵커	news anchor
4과	어머니	mother
4과	어서 오세요	welcome
4과	엄마	mom
4과	연습	practice
4과	연습생	trainee
4과	옛날	past, in the
4과	온라인	online
4과	운동하다	exercise, to
4과	음식	food
4과	음악	music
4과	응원봉	light stick
4과	이야기하다	talk/tell, to
4과	인디 밴드	indie band
4과	인터넷	internet
4과	인터뷰	interview
4과	저녁	evening
4과	춤	dance
4과	콘서트장	concert hall
4과	티켓	ticket
4과	하루 일과	daily routine
4과	혼자	alone
4과	홍보	promotion, advertisment
4과	화장실	bathroom
4과	확인하다	check, to
4과	휴대 전화	mobile phone
4과	힘들다	hard/tough, to be

5과

5과	가족	family
5과	감기	cold (being unwell)
5과	감기약	cold medicine
5과	감기에 걸리다	catch a cold, to
5과	거짓말	lie
5과	걱정하다	worried, to be
5과	기쁘다	happy, to be
5과	깜짝 놀라다	surprised, to be
5과	나가다	exit/go out, to
5과	날씨	weather
5과	넘어지다	fall down, to
5과	눈물	tears
5과	다녀오다	go and come back, to
5과	다치다	get hurt, to
5과	다큐멘터리	documentary
5과	닦다	wipe/brush, to
5과	대단하다	amazing, to be
5과	도시락	lunchbox
5과	동생	younger sibling
5과	동의하다	agree, to
5과	디자인	design
5과	목	neck
5과	무릎	knee
5과	배	stomach
5과	배탈	stomach ache

5과	병원	hospital
5과	부끄럽다	shy/embarassed, to
5과	불편하다	uncomfortable, to be
5과	비타민	vitamin
5과	사다	buy, to
5과	새	new
5과	생일	birthday
5과	서명	signature
5과	선물	present/gift
5과	성명	name and surname
5과	소화제	digestive medicine
5과	스트레칭	stretching
5과	시끄럽다	noisy, to be
5과	아끼다	cherish/value/hold dear, to
5과	아이	child
5과	아프다	sick/unwell, to be; hurt, to
5과	약사	pharmacist
5과	연락처	phone number
5과	열	fever
5과	영국	UK
5과	예쁘다	pretty, to be
5과	예약하다	book/make a reservation, to
5과	올리다	upload (a file), to
5과	요즘	these day/recently
5과	울다	cry, to
5과	의사	doctor
5과	인기가 많다	popular, to be
5과	자전거	bicycle
5과	잠을 자다	sleep, to
5과	장염	stomach flu
5과	접수증	registration card
5과	제품	product
5과	주민등록번호	resident registration number
5과	주소	address
5과	죽	rice porridge
5과	증상	symptom
5과	짜증을 내다	get annoyed, to
5과	코	nose
5과	피곤하다	tired, to be
5과	한강	Han river
5과	헤어지다	break up, to

6과

6과	가게	shop/store
6과	거의	almost
6과	결혼하다	get married, to
6과	경험하다	experience, to
6과	계획	plan/project
6과	고향	hometown
6과	공기 놀이	traditional Korean jacks game
6과	관심	interest
6과	기사	article
6과	까치	magpie
6과	날짜	date (calendar)
6과	너무	too much/very
6과	담배	cigarette
6과	대중교통	public transportation
6과	도착하다	arrive, to
6과	떡국	rice cake soup
6과	똑같다	same, to be the
6과	만두	dumpling
6과	만들다	make, to
6과	멀리	far away
6과	멋있다	cool/stylish, to be
6과	명절	traditional holiday
6과	묻다	ask, to
6과	물건	item/thing
6과	반	half
6과	변경하다	change/modify, to
6과	불교	buddhism
6과	비행기표	plane ticket
6과	사이트	website
6과	설날	lunar new year
6과	세배를 하다	bow (new year greetings), to
6과	세우다	make (a plan), to
6과	송편	traditional rice cake eaten during the lunar new year festivities
6과	쉬다	rest, to
6과	신문	newspaper
6과	쓰다	write, to
6과	연휴	holiday break
6과	올해	this year
6과	외롭다	lonely, to be
6과	윷놀이	traditional Korean game
6과	이동하다	move, to
6과	인구	population
6과	일이 생기다	come up (something), to
6과	읽다	read, to
6과	자꾸	repeatedly
6과	자라다	grow up, to
6과	작년	last year
6과	짓다	build, to
6과	차례를 지내다	perform ancestral rites, to
6과	책	book
6과	체크인	check in
6과	취소하다	cancel, to
6과	치다	play (tennis), to
6과	친척	relatives
6과	테니스	tennis
6과	팔다	sell, to
6과	편안하다	comfortable, to be
6과	피우다	smoke, to
6과	하룻밤	one night
6과	함께	together
6과	해외	overseas/abroad

7과

7과	가능하다	possible, to be
7과	거리	distance
7과	검사	inspection
7과	고민하다	worry, to/concerned, to be
7과	공원	park
7과	구경하다	sightsee, to
7과	군인	soldier
7과	기사님	driver
7과	긴장감	tension
7과	다리	bridge
7과	등산하다	hike, to
7과	따뜻하다	warm, to be
7과	마을	village
7과	맛있다	tasty, to be
7과	매표소	ticket booth
7과	바람	wind
7과	반찬	side dishe
7과	방문객	visitor
7과	배가 부르다	be full (eating), to
7과	번호	number
7과	변하다	change, to
7과	북한	North Korea
7과	불다(바람이)	blow (wind), to
7과	생기다	happen, to
7과	스노보드	snowboard
7과	식당	restaurant
7과	아저씨	mister, middle-aged man
7과	얼굴	face
7과	엄청	very
7과	여러가지	various kinds
7과	완료되다	completed, to be
7과	유료	paid (opposite to free of charge)
7과	자동차	car
7과	전시회	exhibition
7과	젊다	young, to be
7과	찌개	stew
7과	창문	window
7과	체험	experience (hands-on)
7과	춥다	cold, to be
7과	카페	café
7과	특별하다	special, to be
7과	평화	peace
7과	환불	refund
7과	활동	activity

8과

8과	건너다	cross, to
8과	국물	broth
8과	길	street
8과	김치찌개	kimchi stew
8과	끓다	boil, to
8과	남기다	leave (an amount/quantity), to
8과	남자	man/male
8과	냄비	pot
8과	냉면	cold noodles
8과	넣다	put, to
8과	다리	legs
8과	단골	regular customer
8과	댓글	comment (online posting)
8과	데이트	date (romantic)
8과	동네	neighborhood
8과	떡볶이	spicy rice cakes
8과	라면	ramyon
8과	마지막	last
8과	방	room
8과	배달	delivery
8과	볶다	stir fry, to
8과	부탁 드리다	make a request (polite), to
8과	비슷하다	similar, to be
8과	빙수	shaved iced (dessert)
8과	소스	sauce
8과	소울 푸드	soul food
8과	순위	ranking
8과	아이스크림	ice cream
8과	앉다	sit, to
8과	양	quantity
8과	이유	reason
8과	인생	life
8과	자르다	cut, to
8과	자주	often
8과	적다	few, to be
8과	정리하다	tidy up/organise, to
8과	제육볶음	stir-fried spicy pork
8과	주문하다	order, to
8과	중요하다	important, to be
8과	중학생	middle school student
8과	즉석	instant
8과	진짜	really
8과	짜장	black bean sauce
8과	찍다	tap (a card), to
8과	차	tea
8과	차갑다	cold, to be
8과	청소하다	clean, to
8과	최고	best
8과	추가하다	add, to
8과	치즈	cheese
8과	토마트	tomato
8과	팟캐스트	podcast
8과	팬	fan
8과	필수	essential, necessary
8과	항상	always

9과

9과	싸다	cheap, to be
9과	응원하다	cheer, to
9과	즐겁다	joyful, to be
9과	야구장	baseball stadium
9과	경기장	stadium
9과	이메일	email
9과	가입하다	sign up, to
9과	살다	live, to
9과	출근하다	go to work, to
9과	뛰다	run, to
9과	아르바이트	part-time job
9과	방학	holidays (school)
9과	여행	travel/trip
9과	오래되다	old (since something was made), to be
9과	구단	baseball team
9과	경기	game/match
9과	유니폼	uniform
9과	모으다	collect, to
9과	취미	hobby
9과	채널	channel
9과	구매하다	purchase, to
9과	친하다	close (to somebody), to be
9과	머리띠	headband
9과	분위기	atmosphere
9과	응원가	cheer song
9과	부르다	sing, to
9과	즐기다	enjoy, to
9과	치킨	fried chicken
9과	새우	shrimp
9과	튀김	fried (food)
9과	피자	pizza
9과	삼겹살	pork belly
9과	세트	set
9과	다양하다	diverse/various, to be
9과	직접	directly
9과	복잡하다	crowded/complicated, to be
9과	목도리	scarf
9과	조용히	quitely
9과	회오리 감자	tornado potato
9과	성격	personality
9과	긍정적	positive (personality, attitude)
9과	사귀다	make friend/date, to
9과	휴일	holiday/day off
9과	기억하다	remember, to
9과	대만	Taiwan
9과	맵다	spicy, to be
9과	하와이	Hawaii
9과	달리다	run, to
9과	당연히	of course
9과	선수	athlete/player

10과

10과	강연	lecture
10과	겨울	winter
10과	글쎄요	I am not sure/well...
10과	나누다	divide/share, to
10과	단위	unit (of measurement)
10과	들어가다	enter/go in, to
10과	맞다	correct/right, to be
10과	바다	sea
10과	바닷가	beach/seaside
10과	박물관	museum
10과	배우다	learn, to
10과	소설	novel
10과	손	hand
10과	수영하다	swim, to
10과	쉽다	easy, to be
10과	시리즈	series
10과	어린이	little/young, be
10과	여성	female (gender)
10과	여자	female/lady
10과	열심히	diligently
10과	자연	nature
10과	잡다	catch, to
10과	점점	gradually
10과	지키다	protect, to
10과	직업	job/occupation
10과	질문	question
10과	최초	first/original
10과	출처	source
10과	크리스마스	Christmas
10과	한꺼번	all at once
10과	해녀	woman diver
10과	해산물	seafood

Appendix 04: Word list (Korean to English)

ㄱ, ㄲ

가게	shop/store	6과
가격	price	3과
가깝다	near, to be	3과
가끔	sometimes	2과
가능하다	possible, to be	7과
가다	go, to	2과
가방	bag	1과
가수	singer	4과
가운데	middle/centre	3과
가입하다	sign up, to	9과
가져 가다	take (something), to	4과
가족	family	5과
감기	cold (being unwell)	5과
감기약	cold medicine	5과
감기에 걸리다	catch a cold, to	5과
갑자기	suddenly	3과
갓	traditional Korean hat	1과
강연	lecture	10과
개인	individual/personal	1과
거리	distance	7과
거의	almost	6과
거짓말	lie	5과
걱정하다	worried, to be	5과
건너다	cross, to	8과
건축	architecture	1과
걷다	walk, to	4과
걸다	hang, to	4과
검사	inspection	7과
검색하다	search, to	1과
겨울	winter	10과
결혼하다	get married, to	6과
경기	game/match	9과
경기장	stadium	9과
경험하다	experience, to	6과
계획	plan/project	6과
고글	goggles	3과
고등학생	high school student	4과
고르다	choose/select, to	3과
고맙다	thankful, be	1과
고민하다	worry, to/concerned, to be	7과
고향	hometown	6과
공기 놀이	traditional Korean jacks game	6과
공부하다	study, to	4과
공연	show/performance	4과
공원	park	7과
공지 사항	announcement/notice	1과
공짜	free of charge	1과
관람	viewing/watching (an exhibition)	1과
관심	interest	6과
괜찮다	okay/fine, to be	2과
구경하다	sightsee, to	7과
구단	baseball team	9과
구매하다	purchase, to	9과
국가	country	3과
국물	broth	8과
국제특급	international express	2과
군인	soldier	7과
굿즈 부스	merchandise booth	4과
그래서	then	1과
그룹	group	4과
그리고	and	1과
근처	nearby	3과
글쎄요	I am not sure/well...	10과
긍정적	positive (personality, attitude)	9과
기대하다	expect, to	1과
기쁘다	happy, to be	5과
기사	article	6과
기사님	driver	7과
기억하다	remember, to	9과
기차역	train station	3과
기차표	train ticket	3과
긴장감	tension	7과
길	street	8과
김치찌개	kimchi stew	8과
까치	magpie	6과
깜짝 놀라다	surprised, to be	5과
깨끗하다	clean, to be	3과
꽃신	traditional decorated Korean shoes	1과
끓다	boil, to	8과
끝나다	finish, to	2과

ㄴ

나가다	exit/go out, to	5과
나누다	divide/share, to	10과
나오다	appear/come out, to	4과
나이	age	2과
나중에	later	3과
날씨	weather	5과
날짜	date (calendar)	6과
남기다	leave (an amount/quantity), to	8과
남다	left, to be	1과
남색	navy	1과

남자	man/male	8과
내국인	domestic person	1과
내다	pay, to	1과
내리다	get off, to	4과
냄비	pot	8과
냉면	cold noodles	8과
너무	too much/very	6과
넓다	wide/spacious, to be	3과
넘어지다	fall down, to	5과
넣다	put, to	8과
노란색	yellow	1과
노래	song	4과
놀다	play/hang out, to	3과
높다	high/tall, be	2과
누구	who	2과
눈물	tears	5과
늦다	late, to be	1과

ㄷ, ㄸ

다녀오다	go and come back, to	5과
다르다	different, to be	1과
다리	bridge	7과
다리	legs	8과
다시	again	4과
다양하다	diverse/various, to be	9과
다치다	get hurt, to	5과
다큐멘터리	documentary	5과
닦다	wipe/brush, to	5과
단골	regular customer	8과
단위	unit (of measurement)	10과
단체	group	1과
달리다	run, to	9과
닭강정	sweet fried chicken nuggets	3과
담배	cigarette	6과
당연히	of course	9과
대단하다	amazing, to be	5과
대답	answer	4과
대리	assistant manager	2과
대만	Taiwan	9과
대여	rental	1과
대중 가요	pop song	4과
대중교통	public transportation	6과
대표	representative	3과
댓글	comment (online posting)	8과
데이트	date (romantic)	8과
도시락	lunchbox	5과
도착하다	arrive, to	6과
돈	money	1과
돕다	help, to	4과
동네	neighborhood	8과
동생	younger sibling	5과
동영상	video	4과
동의하다	agree, to	5과
두루마기	traditional Korean overcoat	1과
듣다	listen, to	2과
들어가다	enter, to	1과
들어가다	enter/go in, to	10과
등산하다	hike, to	7과
디자인	design	5과
따뜻하다	warm, to be	7과
떡국	rice cake soup	6과
떡볶이	spicy rice cakes	8과
똑같다	same, to be the	6과
뛰다	run, to	9과
뜻	meaning	1과

ㄹ, ㅁ

라면	ramyon	8과
리뷰	review	1과
마시다	drink, to	2과
마을	village	7과
마을 버스	trolley bus	3과
마음에 들다	satisfied/happy with something, to be	1과
마이크	microphone	1과
마지막	last	8과
막히다	blocked/jammed, to be	2과
만나다	meet, to	1과
만두	dumpling	6과
만들다	make, to	6과
많다	many, to be	1과
말실수	slip of the tongue	2과
말씀하다	speak, to (polite)	4과
말하다	speak/say, to	1과
맛있다	tasty, to be	7과
맞다	correct/right, to be	10과
맡기다	leave/deposit, to	1과
매일	every day	1과
매점	store	4과
매표소	ticket booth	7과
맵다	spicy, to be	9과
머리띠	headband	9과
먹다	eat, to	2과
먼저	first, in advance	1과
멀리	far away	6과
멈추다	stop, to	3과
멋있다	cool/stylish, to be	6과
명절	traditional holiday	6과
모르다	not know, to	3과
모으다	collect, to	9과
모임	gathering	2과
모자	hat/cap	3과
목	neck	5과
목도리	scarf	9과
무료	free of charge	1과
무릎	knee	5과

문화	culture	2과
묻다	ask, to	6과
물건	item/thing	6과
미국	US	4과
미리	in advance	3과

ㅂ, ㅃ

바다	sea	10과
바닷가	beach/seaside	10과
바람	wind	7과
바지	pants	1과
박물관	museum	10과
반	half	6과
반갑다	glad, to be	4과
반말	informal speech	2과
반찬	side dishe	7과
받다	receive, to	1과
밤	night	4과
밥	rice/meal	2과
방	room	8과
방금	just now	4과
방문객	visitor	7과
방송	broadcast	4과
방학	holidays (school)	9과
배	stomach	5과
배가 부르다	be full (eating), to	7과
배달	delivery	8과
배우	actor/actress	4과
배우다	learn, to	10과
배탈	stomach ache	5과
버컬	vocal	4과
번호	number	7과
베트남	Vietnam	3과
변경하다	change/modify, to	6과
변하다	change, to	7과
별로	not really (used with negative verbs)	3과
병원	hospital	5과
보관함	storage cabinet	1과
보내다	send, to	2과
보라색	purple	1과
보물	treasure	4과
보이다	seen, to be	3과
보통	usually	4과
복잡하다	crowded/complicated, to be	9과
볶다	stir fry, to	8과
부끄럽다	shy/embarassed, to	5과
부르다	sing, to	9과
부츠	boots	3과
부탁 드리다	make a request (polite), to	8과
북한	North Korea	7과
분위기	atmosphere	9과
불교	buddhism	6과

불다(바람이)	blow (wind), to	7과
불편하다	uncomfortable, to be	5과
비슷하다	similar, to be	8과
비싸다	expensive, to be	1과
비자	visa	3과
비타민	vitamin	5과
비행기표	plane ticket	6과
빌리다	borrow, to	2과
빙수	shaved iced (dessert)	8과
빠르다	quick/fast, to be	2과
빨간색	red	1과

ㅅ, ㅆ

사고	accident	3과
사귀다	make friend/date, to	9과
사다	buy, to	5과
사람	people	1과
사용하다	use, to	4과
사우나	sauna	3과
사이트	website	6과
사장님	boss	2과
사진	photo	1과
산	mountain	2과
살다	live, to	9과
삼겹살	pork belly	9과
새	new	5과
새롭다	new, to be	4과
새우	shrimp	9과
생기다	happen, to	7과
생일	birthday	5과
생활	life	2과
서명	signature	5과
선물	present/gift	5과
선수	athlete/player	9과
선택하다	choose/select, to	3과
설날	lunar new year	6과
성격	personality	9과
성명	name and surname	5과
세배를 하다	bow (new year greetings), to	6과
세우다	make (a plan), to	6과
세트	set	9과
셔틀버스	shuttle bus	3과
소개하다	introduce, to	4과
소설	novel	10과
소속사	entertainment company, agency	4과
소스	sauce	8과
소울 푸드	soul food	8과
소화제	digestive medicine	5과
손	hand	10과
송편	traditional rice cake eaten during the lunar new year festivities	6과
수업	class	4과
수영하다	swim, to	10과

숙박 시설	accommodation	3과
순위	ranking	8과
술	alcohol	2과
쉬다	rest, to	6과
쉽다	easy, to be	10과
스노보드	snowboard	7과
스키	ski	3과
스키장	ski resort	3과
스트레칭	stretching	5과
스페인어	Spanish language	1과
스피치	speech	4과
시간	time	1과
시끄럽다	noisy, to be	5과
시리즈	series	10과
시작하다	start, to	1과
시키다	order, to	3과
식당	restaurant	7과
식사하다	have a meal, to	2과
신나다	excited, to be	1과
신다	wear (shoes), to	1과
신문	newspaper	6과
신분증	ID card	3과
신입 사원	new employee	2과
싸다	cheap, to be	9과
쓰다	wear (hat/cap), to	1과
쓰다	write, to	6과

ㅇ

아끼다	cherish/value/hold dear, to	5과
아르바이트	part-time job	9과
아이	child	5과
아이돌	idol	4과
아이스크림	ice cream	8과
아저씨	mister, middle-aged man	7과
아주머니	ma'am	3과
아침	morning	4과
아프다	sick/unwell, to be; hurt, to	5과
안내	information	1과
안전	safety	3과
앉다	sit, to	8과
알다	know, to	1과
알리다	inform/let know, to	3과
앵커	news anchor	4과
야간	night time	3과
야구	baseball	3과
야구장	baseball stadium	9과
약사	pharmacist	5과
약속	appointment, promise	1과
양	quantity	8과
어렵다	difficult, to be	2과
어린이	little/young, be	10과
어머니	mother	4과
어서 오세요	welcome	4과
언어	language	1과
얼굴	face	7과
얼른	quickly	3과
엄마	mom	4과
엄청	very	7과
여권	passport	3과
여러가지	various kinds	7과
여성	female (gender)	10과
여자	female/lady	10과
여행	travel/trip	9과
연락처	phone number	5과
연습	practice	4과
연습생	trainee	4과
연휴	holiday break	6과
열	fever	5과
열심히	diligently	10과
영국	UK	5과
영상	video	1과
영어	English language	1과
영화	film	3과
예쁘다	pretty, to be	5과
예약하다	book/make a reservation, to	5과
옛날	past, in the	4과
오래되다	old (since something was made), to be	9과
오전	morning	3과
오후	afternoon	3과
온라인	online	4과
올리다	upload (a file), to	5과
올해	this year	6과
옷	dress/clothes	1과
완료되다	completed, to be	7과
외국인	foreign person	1과
외롭다	lonely, to be	6과
요금	fee/charge	1과
요즘	these day/recently	5과
우체국	post office	2과
운동하다	exercise, to	4과
울다	cry, to	5과
움직이다	move, to	3과
웃다	laugh/smile, to	2과
원래	originally	2과
위험하다	dangerous, to be	3과
유니폼	uniform	9과
유료	paid (opposite to free of charge)	7과
유튜브	YouTube	1과
윷놀이	traditional Korean game	6과
음식	food	4과
음악	music	4과

응원가	cheer song	9과
응원봉	light stick	4과
응원하다	cheer, to	9과
의사	doctor	5과
이동하다	move, to	6과
이따가	later (usually within the same day)	3과
이메일	email	9과
이야기하다	talk/tell, to	4과
이용 시간	operating hours	3과
이유	reason	8과
이해하다	understand, to	2과
인구	population	6과
인기가 많다	popular, to be	5과
인디 밴드	indie band	4과
인생	life	8과
인터넷	internet	4과
인터뷰	interview	4과
일이 생기다	come up (something), to	6과
일찍	early	1과
일하다	work, to	2과
읽다	read, to	6과
입다	wear, to	1과
입장	admission	1과

ㅈ, ㅉ

자꾸	repeatedly	6과
자동차	car	7과
자라다	grow up, to	6과
자르다	cut, to	8과
자세하다	detailed, to be	2과
자연	nature	10과
자전거	bicycle	5과
자주	often	8과
작년	last year	6과
잘하다	do well, to	2과
잠을 자다	sleep, to	5과
잡다	catch, to	10과
장갑	gloves	3과
장비	equipment	3과
장소	place	3과
장염	stomach flu	5과
재미있다	interesting/fun, to be	2과
저고리	traditional Korean jacket	1과
저녁	evening	4과
적다	few, to be	8과
전시회	exhibition	7과
전통	tradition/traditional	1과
젊다	young, to be	7과
점심	lunch	2과
점점	gradually	10과

접수증	registration card	5과
정리하다	tidy up/organise, to	8과
정말	really	1과
제육볶음	stir-fried spicy pork	8과
제품	product	5과
조금	a little	1과
조심하다	careful, to be	3과
조용히	quitely	9과
존댓말	formal language	2과
좋다	good, to be	2과
주말	weekend	1과
주문하다	order, to	8과
주민등록번호	resident registration number	5과
주소	address	5과
주의 사항	precautions	3과
주황색	orange	1과
죽	rice porridge	5과
준비 운동	warm-up exercise	3과
준비하다	prepare, to	3과
중요하다	important, to be	8과
중학생	middle school student	8과
즉석	instant	8과
즐겁다	joyful, to be	9과
즐기다	enjoy, to	9과
증상	symptom	5과
지금	now	3과
지키다	protect, to	10과
지하철	subway	1과
직업	job/occupation	10과
직원	employee	3과
직접	directly	9과
진짜	really	8과
질문	question	10과
짓다	build, to	6과
짜장	black bean sauce	8과
짜증을 내다	get annoyed, to	5과
찌개	stew	7과
찍다	take (a photo/a video), to	1과
찍다	tap (a card), to	8과

ㅊ

차	tea	8과
차갑다	cold, to be	8과
차례를 지내다	perform ancestral rites, to	6과
착용	wear, to	1과
참석하다	attend, to	2과
참치	tuna	3과
창문	window	7과
찾다	find/look for, to	1과
채널	channel	9과

책	book	6과
처음	first/beginning	2과
청소하다	clean, to	8과
체크인	check in	6과
체험	experience (hands-on)	7과
초록색	green	1과
최고	best	8과
최초	first/original	10과
추가하다	add, to	8과
추천하다	suggest, to	2과
축제	festival	3과
축하하다	congratulate, to	2과
출근하다	go to work, to	9과
출처	source	10과
춤	dance	4과
춥다	cold, to be	7과
취미	hobby	9과
취소하다	cancel, to	6과
취직하다	get a job, to	2과
치다	play (tennis), to	6과
치마	skirt	1과
치즈	cheese	8과
치킨	fried chicken	9과
친구	friend	3과
친절하다	kind, to be	2과
친척	relatives	6과
친하다	close (to somebody), to be	9과

ㅋ, ㅌ

카페	café	7과
케이크	cake	3과
코	nose	5과
콘서트장	concert hall	4과
콜라	coke	2과
크리스마스	Christmas	10과
큰일 나다	serious, be (said of a situation)	1과
타다	take (a mean of transportation), to	1과
탈의실	change room	1과
택시	taxi	3과
테니스	tennis	6과
토마토	tomato	8과
튀김	fried (food)	9과
특별하다	special, to be	7과
특히	especially/in particular	2과
티켓	ticket	4과

ㅍ

파란색	blue	1과
파일	file (computer)	1과

팔다	sell, to	6과
팟캐스트	podcast	8과
팬	fan	8과
편안하다	comfortable, to be	6과
편하다	comfortable, to be	2과
평일	weekday	3과
평화	peace	7과
포스터	poster	3과
프랑스어	French language	1과
프로젝트	project	2과
피곤하다	tired, to be	5과
피우다	smoke, to	6과
피자	pizza	9과
필수	essential, necessary	8과

ㅎ

하루	a day/one day	1과
하루 일과	daily routine	4과
하룻밤	one night	6과
하얀색	white	1과
하와이	Hawaii	9과
한강	Han river	5과
한꺼번	all at once	10과
한반도	Korean peninsula	2과
한복	Korean traditional dress	1과
할머니	grandmother	2과
함께	together	6과
항상	always	8과
해녀	woman diver	10과
해산물	seafood	10과
해외	overseas/abroad	6과
헤어지다	break up, to	5과
헬멧	helmet	3과
형	older brother	2과
호주	Australia	2과
혹시	perhaps	3과
혼자	alone	4과
홍보	promotion, advertisment	4과
화장실	bathroom	4과
확인하다	check, to	4과
환불	refund	7과
환영하다	welcome, to	2과
환영회	welcome party	2과
활동	activity	7과
회식	company dinner	2과
회오리 감자	tornado potato	9과
횡단보도	zebra crossing	3과
휴대 전화	mobile phone	4과
휴일	holiday/day off	9과
힘들다	hard/tough, to be	4과

Appendix 05: Word list (English to Korean)

A

English	Korean	Lesson
a day/one day	하루	1과
a little	조금	1과
accident	사고	3과
accommodation	숙박 시설	3과
activity	활동	7과
actor/actress	배우	4과
add, to	추가하다	8과
address	주소	5과
admission	입장	1과
afternoon	오후	3과
again	다시	4과
age	나이	2과
agree, to	동의하다	5과
alcohol	술	2과
all at once	한꺼번	10과
almost	거의	6과
alone	혼자	4과
always	항상	8과
amazing, to be	대단하다	5과
and	그리고	1과
announcement/notice	공지 사항	1과
answer	대답	4과
appear/come out, to	나오다	4과
appointment, promise	약속	1과
architecture	건축	1과
arrive, to	도착하다	6과
article	기사	6과
ask, to	묻다	6과
assistant manager	대리	2과
athlete/player	선수	9과
atmosphere	분위기	9과
attend, to	참석하다	2과
Australia	호주	2과

B

English	Korean	Lesson
bag	가방	1과
baseball	야구	3과
baseball stadium	야구장	9과
baseball team	구단	9과
bathroom	화장실	4과
be full (eating), to	배가 부르다	7과
beach/seaside	바닷가	10과
best	최고	8과
bicycle	자전거	5과
birthday	생일	5과
black bean sauce	짜장	8과
blocked/jammed, to be	막히다	2과
blow (wind), to	불다(바람이)	7과
blue	파란색	1과
boil, to	끓다	8과
book	책	6과
book/make a reservation, to	예약하다	5과
boots	부츠	3과
borrow, to	빌리다	2과
boss	사장님	2과
bow (new year greetings), to	세배를 하다	6과
break up, to	헤어지다	5과
bridge	다리	7과
broadcast	방송	4과
broth	국물	8과
buddhism	불교	6과
build, to	짓다	6과
buy, to	사다	5과

C

English	Korean	Lesson
café	카페	7과
cake	케이크	3과
cancel, to	취소하다	6과
car	자동차	7과
careful, to be	조심하다	3과
catch a cold, to	감기에 걸리다	5과
catch, to	잡다	10과
change room	탈의실	1과
change, to	변하다	7과
change/modify, to	변경하다	6과
channel	채널	9과
cheap, to be	싸다	9과
check in	체크인	6과
check, to	확인하다	4과
cheer song	응원가	9과
cheer, to	응원하다	9과
cheese	치즈	8과
cherish/value/hold dear, to	아끼다	5과
child	아이	5과
choose/select, to	고르다	3과
choose/select, to	선택하다	3과
Christmas	크리스마스	10과
cigarette	담배	6과
class	수업	4과
clean, to	청소하다	8과

English	Korean	과
clean, to be	깨끗하다	3과
close (to somebody), to be	친하다	9과
coke	콜라	2과
cold (being unwell)	감기	5과
cold medicine	감기약	5과
cold noodles	냉면	8과
cold, to be	차갑다	8과
cold, to be	춥다	7과
collect, to	모으다	9과
come up (something), to	일이 생기다	6과
comfortable, to be	편안하다	6과
comfortable, to be	편하다	2과
comment (online posting)	댓글	8과
company dinner	회식	2과
completed, to be	완료되다	7과
concert hall	콘서트장	4과
congratulate, to	축하하다	2과
cool/stylish, to be	멋있다	6과
correct/right, to be	맞다	10과
country	국가	3과
cross, to	건너다	8과
crowded/complicated, to be	복잡하다	9과
cry, to	울다	5과
culture	문화	2과
cut, to	자르다	8과

D

English	Korean	과
daily routine	하루 일과	4과
dance	춤	4과
dangerous, to be	위험하다	3과
date (calendar)	날짜	6과
date (romantic)	데이트	8과
delivery	배달	8과
design	디자인	5과
detailed, to be	자세하다	2과
different, to be	다르다	1과
difficult, to be	어렵다	2과
digestive medicine	소화제	5과
diligently	열심히	10과
directly	직접	9과
distance	거리	7과
diverse/various, to be	다양하다	9과
divide/share, to	나누다	10과
do well, to	잘하다	2과
doctor	의사	5과
documentary	다큐멘터리	5과
domestic person	내국인	1과
dress/clothes	옷	1과
drink, to	마시다	2과
driver	기사님	7과
dumpling	만두	6과

E

English	Korean	과
early	일찍	1과
easy, to be	쉽다	10과
eat, to	먹다	2과
email	이메일	9과
employee	직원	3과
English language	영어	1과
enjoy, to	즐기다	9과
enter, to	들어가다	1과
enter/go in, to	들어가다	10과
entertainment company, agency	소속사	4과
equipment	장비	3과
especially/in particular	특히	2과
essential, necessary	필수	8과
evening	저녁	4과
every day	매일	1과
excited, to be	신나다	1과
exercise, to	운동하다	4과
exhibition	전시회	7과
exit/go out, to	나가다	5과
expect, to	기대하다	1과
expensive, to be	비싸다	1과
experience (hands-on)	체험	7과
experience, to	경험하다	6과

F

English	Korean	과
face	얼굴	7과
fall down, to	넘어지다	5과
family	가족	5과
fan	팬	8과
far away	멀리	6과
fee/charge	요금	1과
female (gender)	여성	10과
female/lady	여자	10과
festival	축제	3과
fever	열	5과
few, to be	적다	8과
file (computer)	파일	1과
film	영화	3과
find/look for, to	찾다	1과
finish, to	끝나다	2과
first, in advance	먼저	1과
first/beginning	처음	2과
first/original	최초	10과
food	음식	4과
foreign person	외국인	1과
formal language	존댓말	2과
free of charge	공짜	1과
free of charge	무료	1과
French language	프랑스어	1과

English	Korean	Lesson
fried (food)	튀김	9과
fried chicken	치킨	9과
friend	친구	3과

G

English	Korean	Lesson
game/match	경기	9과
gathering	모임	2과
get a job, to	취직하다	2과
get annoyed, to	짜증을 내다	5과
get hurt, to	다치다	5과
get married, to	결혼하다	6과
get off, to	내리다	4과
glad, to be	반갑다	4과
gloves	장갑	3과
go and come back, to	다녀오다	5과
go to work, to	출근하다	9과
go, to	가다	2과
goggles	고글	3과
good, to be	좋다	2과
gradually	점점	10과
grandmother	할머니	2과
green	초록색	1과
group	그룹	4과
group	단체	1과
grow up, to	자라다	6과

H

English	Korean	Lesson
half	반	6과
Han river	한강	5과
hand	손	10과
hang, to	걸다	4과
happen, to	생기다	7과
happy, to be	기쁘다	5과
hard/tough, to be	힘들다	4과
hat/cap	모자	3과
have a meal, to	식사하다	2과
Hawaii	하와이	9과
headband	머리띠	9과
helmet	헬멧	3과
help, to	돕다	4과
high school student	고등학생	4과
high/tall, be	높다	2과
hike, to	등산하다	7과
hobby	취미	9과
holiday break	연휴	6과
holiday/day off	휴일	9과
holidays (school)	방학	9과
hometown	고향	6과
hospital	병원	5과

I

English	Korean	Lesson
I am not sure/well...	글쎄요	10과
ice cream	아이스크림	8과
ID card	신분증	3과
idol	아이돌	4과
important, to be	중요하다	8과
in advance	미리	3과
indie band	인디 밴드	4과
individual/personal	개인	1과
inform/let know, to	알리다	3과
informal speech	반말	2과
information	안내	1과
inspection	검사	7과
instant	즉석	8과
interest	관심	6과
interesting/fun, to be	재미있다	2과
international express	국제특급	2과
internet	인터넷	4과
interview	인터뷰	4과
introduce, to	소개하다	4과
item/thing	물건	6과

J, K

English	Korean	Lesson
job/occupation	직업	10과
joyful, to be	즐겁다	9과
just now	방금	4과
kimchi stew	김치찌개	8과
kind, to be	친절하다	2과
knee	무릎	5과
know, to	알다	1과
Korean peninsula	한반도	2과
Korean traditional dress	한복	1과

L

English	Korean	Lesson
language	언어	1과
last	마지막	8과
last year	작년	6과
late, to be	늦다	1과
later	나중에	3과
later (usually within the same day)	이따가	3과
laugh/smile, to	웃다	2과
learn, to	배우다	10과
leave (an amount/quantity), to	남기다	8과
leave/deposit, to	맡기다	1과
lecture	강연	10과
left, to be	남다	1과
legs	다리	8과

English	Korean	과
lie	거짓말	5과
life	생활	2과
life	인생	8과
light stick	응원봉	4과
listen, to	듣다	2과
little/young, be	어린이	10과
live, to	살다	9과
lonely, to be	외롭다	6과
lunar new year	설날	6과
lunch	점심	2과
lunchbox	도시락	5과

M

English	Korean	과
ma'am	아주머니	3과
magpie	까치	6과
make (a plan), to	세우다	6과
make a request (polite), to	부탁 드리다	8과
make friend/date, to	사귀다	9과
make, to	만들다	6과
man/male	남자	8과
many, to be	많다	1과
meaning	뜻	1과
meet, to	만나다	1과
merchandise booth	굿즈 부스	4과
microphone	마이크	1과
middle school student	중학생	8과
middle/centre	가운데	3과
mister, middle-aged man	아저씨	7과
mobile phone	휴대 전화	4과
mom	엄마	4과
money	돈	1과
morning	아침	4과
morning	오전	3과
mother	어머니	4과
mountain	산	2과
move, to	움직이다	3과
move, to	이동하다	6과
museum	박물관	10과
music	음악	4과

N

English	Korean	과
name and surname	성명	5과
nature	자연	10과
navy	남색	1과
near, to be	가깝다	3과
nearby	근처	3과
neck	목	5과
neighborhood	동네	8과
new	새	5과
new employee	신입 사원	2과
new, to be	새롭다	4과
news anchor	앵커	4과
newspaper	신문	6과
night	밤	4과
night time	야간	3과
noisy, to be	시끄럽다	5과
North Korea	북한	7과
nose	코	5과
not know, to	모르다	3과
not really (used with negative verbs)	별로	3과
novel	소설	10과
now	지금	3과
number	번호	7과

O

English	Korean	과
of course	당연히	9과
often	자주	8과
okay/fine, to be	괜찮다	2과
old (since something was made), to be	오래되다	9과
older brother	형	2과
one night	하룻밤	6과
online	온라인	4과
operating hours	이용 시간	3과
orange	주황색	1과
order, to	시키다	3과
order, to	주문하다	8과
originally	원래	2과
overseas/abroad	해외	6과

P

English	Korean	과
paid (opposite to free of charge)	유료	7과
pants	바지	1과
park	공원	7과
part-time job	아르바이트	9과
passport	여권	3과
past, in the	옛날	4과
pay, to	내다	1과
peace	평화	7과
people	사람	1과
perform ancestral rites, to	차례를 지내다	6과
perhaps	혹시	3과
personality	성격	9과
pharmacist	약사	5과
phone number	연락처	5과
photo	사진	1과
pizza	피자	9과

English	Korean	Lesson
place	장소	3과
plan/project	계획	6과
plane ticket	비행기표	6과
play (tennis), to	치다	6과
play/hang out, to	놀다	3과
podcast	팟캐스트	8과
pop song	대중 가요	4과
popular, to be	인기가 많다	5과
population	인구	6과
pork belly	삼겹살	9과
positive (personality, attitude)	긍정적	9과
possible, to be	가능하다	7과
post office	우체국	2과
poster	포스터	3과
pot	냄비	8과
practice	연습	4과
precautions	주의 사항	3과
prepare, to	준비하다	3과
present/gift	선물	5과
pretty, to be	예쁘다	5과
price	가격	3과
product	제품	5과
project	프로젝트	2과
promotion, advertisement	홍보	4과
protect, to	지키다	10과
public transportation	대중교통	6과
purchase, to	구매하다	9과
purple	보라색	1과
put, to	넣다	8과

Q

English	Korean	Lesson
quantity	양	8과
question	질문	10과
quick/fast, to be	빠르다	2과
quickly	얼른	3과
quitely	조용히	9과

R

English	Korean	Lesson
ramyon	라면	8과
ranking	순위	8과
read, to	읽다	6과
really	정말	1과
really	진짜	8과
reason	이유	8과
receive, to	받다	1과
red	빨간색	1과
refund	환불	7과
registration card	접수증	5과
regular customer	단골	8과
relatives	친척	6과
remember, to	기억하다	9과
rental	대여	1과
repeatedly	자꾸	6과
representative	대표	3과
resident registration number	주민등록번호	5과
rest, to	쉬다	6과
restaurant	식당	7과
review	리뷰	1과
rice cake soup	떡국	6과
rice porridge	죽	5과
rice/meal	밥	2과
room	방	8과
run, to	달리다	9과
run, to	뛰다	9과

S

English	Korean	Lesson
safety	안전	3과
same, to be the	똑같다	6과
satisfied/happy with something, to be	마음에 들다	1과
sauce	소스	8과
sauna	사우나	3과
scarf	목도리	9과
sea	바다	10과
seafood	해산물	10과
search, to	검색하다	1과
seen, to be	보이다	3과
sell, to	팔다	6과
send, to	보내다	2과
series	시리즈	10과
serious, be (said of a situation)	큰일나다	1과
set	세트	9과
shaved iced (dessert)	빙수	8과
shop/store	가게	6과
show/performance	공연	4과
shrimp	새우	9과
shuttle bus	셔틀버스	3과
shy/embarassed, to	부끄럽다	5과
sick/unwell, to be; hurt, to	아프다	5과
side dishe	반찬	7과
sightsee, to	구경하다	7과
sign up, to	가입하다	9과
signature	서명	5과
similar, to be	비슷하다	8과
sing, to	부르다	9과
singer	가수	4과
sit, to	앉다	8과
ski	스키	3과
ski resort	스키장	3과

English	Korean	Lesson
skirt	치마	1과
sleep, to	잠을 자다	5과
slip of the tongue	말실수	2과
smoke, to	피우다	6과
snowboard	스노보드	7과
soldier	군인	7과
sometimes	가끔	2과
song	노래	4과
soul food	소울 푸드	8과
source	출처	10과
Spanish language	스페인어	1과
speak, to (polite)	말씀하다	4과
speak/say, to	말하다	1과
special, to be	특별하다	7과
speech	스피치	4과
spicy rice cakes	떡볶이	8과
spicy, to be	맵다	9과
stadium	경기장	9과
start, to	시작하다	1과
stew	찌개	7과
stir fry, to	볶다	8과
stir-fried spicy pork	제육볶음	8과
stomach ache	배탈	5과
stomach	배	5과
stomach flu	장염	5과
stop, to	멈추다	3과
storage cabinet	보관함	1과
store	매점	4과
street	길	8과
stretching	스트레칭	5과
study, to	공부하다	4과
subway	지하철	1과
suddenly	갑자기	3과
suggest, to	추천하다	2과
surprised, to be	깜짝 놀라다	5과
sweet fried chicken nuggets	닭강정	3과
swim, to	수영하다	10과
symptom	증상	5과

T

English	Korean	Lesson
Taiwan	대만	9과
take (a mean of transportation), to	타다	1과
take (a photo/a video), to	찍다	1과
take (something), to	가져 가다	4과
talk/tell, to	이야기하다	4과
tap (a card), to	찍다	8과
tasty, to be	맛있다	7과
taxi	택시	3과
tea	차	8과
tears	눈물	5과
tennis	테니스	6과
tension	긴장감	7과
thankful, be	고맙다	1과
then	그래서	1과
these day/recently	요즘	5과
this year	올해	6과
ticket	티켓	4과
ticket booth	매표소	7과
tidy up/organise, to	정리하다	8과
time	시간	1과
tired, to be	피곤하다	5과
together	함께	6과
tomato	토마토	8과
too much/very	너무	6과
tornado potato	회오리 감자	9과
tradition/traditional	전통	1과
traditional decorated Korean shoes	꽃신	1과
traditional holiday	명절	6과
traditional Korean game	윷놀이	6과
traditional Korean hat	갓	1과
traditional Korean jacket	저고리	1과
traditional Korean jacks game	공기 놀이	6과
traditional Korean overcoat	두루마기	1과
traditional rice cake eaten during the lunar new year festivities	송편	6과
train station	기차역	3과
train ticket	기차표	3과
trainee	연습생	4과
travel/trip	여행	9과
treasure	보물	4과
trolley bus	마을 버스	3과
tuna	참치	3과

U, V

English	Korean	Lesson
UK	영국	5과
uncomfortable, to be	불편하다	5과
understand, to	이해하다	2과
uniform	유니폼	9과
unit (of measurement)	단위	10과
upload (a file), to	올리다	5과
US	미국	4과
use, to	사용하다	4과
usually	보통	4과
various kinds	여러가지	7과
very	엄청	7과
video	동영상	4과
video	영상	1과
Vietnam	베트남	3과

English	Korean	Lesson
viewing/watching (an exhibition)	관람	1과
village	마을	7과
visa	비자	3과
visitor	방문객	7과
vitamin	비타민	5과
vocal	버컬	4과

W

English	Korean	Lesson
walk, to	걷다	4과
warm-up exercise	준비 운동	3과
warm, to be	따뜻하다	7과
wear (hat/cap), to	쓰다	1과
wear (shoes), to	신다	1과
wear, to	입다	1과
wear, to	착용	1과
weather	날씨	5과
website	사이트	6과
weekday	평일	3과
weekend	주말	1과
welcome	어서 오세요	4과
welcome party	환영회	2과
welcome, to	환영하다	2과
white	하얀색	1과
who	누구	2과
wide/spacious, to be	넓다	3과
wind	바람	7과
window	창문	7과
winter	겨울	10과
wipe/brush, to	닦다	5과
woman diver	해녀	10과
work, to	일하다	2과
worried, to be	걱정하다	5과
worry, to/concerned, to be	고민하다	7과
write, to	쓰다	6과

Y, Z

English	Korean	Lesson
yellow	노란색	1과
young, to be	젊다	7과
younger sibling	동생	5과
YouTube	유튜브	1과
zebra crossing	횡단보도	3과

Appendix 06 — Answers to exercises

1과

Pre-reading activity	갓 – 쓰다; 한복/저고리/치마/바지/두루마기 – 입다; 꽃신 – 신다 1. 입었어요/입을 거예요; 2. 썼어요; 3. 입었어요; 4. 신을 거예요
Reading	A) 2,3; B) 1.프랑스어 안내 서비스를 시작해요; 2. 한국어, 영어, 일본어, 중국어 안내 서비스를 받을 수 있어요; 3. 프랑스어를 시작할 거예요; 4. 다음 달부터 매주 수요일하고 목요일 오전 11시와 오후 3시에 받을 수 있어요.
Pre-listening activity	파란색 – blue; 하얀색 – white; 노란색 – yellow; 주황색 – orange; 빨간색 – red; 초록색 – green; 보라색 – purple; 남색 – navy 1. 파란색, 흰색; 2. 입었어요; 3. 노란색, 치마, 보라색; 4. 썼어요, 신었어요
Listening activity	A) 1, 4; B) 1. 늦게 가면 한복 머리 스타일링을 많이 기다려야 할 거예요. 2. 늦게 가면 예쁜 옷이 많이 없을 거예요

2과

Pre-reading activity	참석 – 모임이 있어요. 그럼 거기에 가요; 자세하다 – A부터 Z까지 알 수 있어요; 환영하다 – 여러분이 회사에 처음 왔어요. 그럼 회사 사람들이 축하해줘요; 신입 사원 – 저는 며칠 전에 이 회사에 취직했어요.
Reading	A) 1. 우리 신입 사원이잖아; 2. 이번 회식은 신입 사원 환영회잖아; 3. 저 술을 못 마시는데…; 4. 요즘엔 사람들이 술을 많이 안 마셔; 5. 회식이 생각보다 재미있을 거야; 6. 이번 회식은 9시에 끝나; B) 1. 회사 사람들하고 저녁에 다 같이 식사해요. 그리고 가끔 같이 노래방에도 가요.
Pre-listening activity	2. 반말; 3. 이해해 줘요; 4. 이렇게 말했어요
Listening activity	A) 2, 4; B) 1. 지난 번에 대리님께 반말했는데 이해해 줬어요; 2. 반말했어요. "밥 잘 먹었어?" 이렇게 말했어요; 3. 존댓말이 제일 어려워요; 4. 할머니께서 사랑 씨를 제일 잘 이해해 주세요; 5. 사랑 씨도 우미드 씨하고 비슷한 말실수를 했어요/사랑 씨가 할머니께 반말했어요; C) 도착하셨어요

3과

Pre-reading activity	안전 – 안 위험해요. 사고가 없어요; 착용하다 – 모자를 써요. 신발을 신어요. 장갑을 껴요; 선택하다 – 어떤 것을 골라야 해요; 멈추다 – 갑자기 안 움직여요
Reading	A) 3, 5; B) 1. 준비운동을 해야 해요; 2. 헬멧하고 보호대를 착용해야 해요; 그럼 덜 위험해요/조금 더 안전해요; 3. 그럼 쉬운 슬로프를 선택해야 해요
Pre-listening activity	1. 셔틀버스를 태야 해요; 2. 뭐가 좋아요; 더 많고 숙박 시설이 좋아요
Listening activity	A) 1; B) 1. (잠실에서) 스키장 버스 타고 왔어; 2. 매점 아주머니께 물어 봤어; C) 다른 스키장보다 셔틀버스가 많아; 숙박 시설이 넓고 깨끗해; 숙박 가격이 다른 곳보다 싸

4과

Pre-reading activity	홍보 – 사람들한테 소개해요; 하루 일과 – 아침부터 저녁까지의 스케줄이에요; 단체 연습 – 다 같이 함께 연습해요; 개인 연습 – 혼자서 연습해요; 소속사 – 가수나 배우의 회사예요
Reading	A) 1, 4, 5; B) 1. 새로운 노래를 홍보하러/소개하러 나왔습니다; 2. 운동을 합니다; 외국어 공부를 합니다; 점심 식사를 합니다; 스피치 수업을 받습니다; 보컬과 춤 수업을 듣습니다; 단체 연습과 개인 연습을 합니다
Pre-listening activity	1. 버스, ②; 2. 동영상, ③; 3. 문, ①
Listening activity	A) 2 B) 1. 휴대 전화로 사진이나 동영상을 찍을 수 없습니다. 그리고 음식도 먹을 수 없습니다; 2. 아니요. 캐롤라인은 딸이랑 공연을 보러 왔습니다. 하루 어머니는 하루랑 공연을 보러 왔습니다; 3. 캐롤라인 씨 딸은 한국에 놀러 왔습니다; 4. 화장실에 갔습니다; 5. 응원봉은 하루의 보물 1호예요

5과	Pre-reading activity	2. 증상; 3. 부끄러웠어요; 4. 닮았어요; 5. 약사; 6. 감기약; 7. 짜증을 냈어요
	Reading	A) 1. 감기약을 사러 약국에 갔습니다. 2. 어린이의 엄마가 아파요. 그래서 울었습니다; 3. "엄마, 어디가 어떻게 아파요? 이렇게 물어봐요"라고 말했습니다; 4. "아이가 대단해요" 이렇게 생각합니다; 5. 이 사람은 자신이 부끄러웠습니다
	Pre-listening activity	언제부터 아팠어요?; 약을 드셨어요?; 무슨 약을 드셨어요?; 혹시 여행 다녀오셨어요?
	Listening activity	A) 4,5; B) 1. 배가 아프고 열이 많이 나서 병원에 왔어요; 2. 네. 30분 동안 계속 아팠어요; 3. 주말이어서 병원에 못 왔어요; 4. 아니요. 가족들은 안 아파요; C). 약을 먹어야 해요. 그리고 물을 많이 마셔야 해요. 오늘은 밥을 안 먹어야 해요. 내일부터 부드러운 죽을 먹어야 해요.

6과	Pre-reading activity	차례를 지내요; 불교 전통 세배를 해요; 떡국 먹어요; 만두 만들어요; 윷놀이 해요; 공기놀이 해요; 템플스테이 홈페이지(www.templestay.com)에서 자세한 정보를 찾을 수 있어요
	Reading	A) 1. "취직했어?"; "언제 결혼할 거야?"; "여자 친구 있어?" 이런 거 물어 봐요; 2. 마음에 들어요/좋아요; 3. 서울에서 가까워서 마곡사로 결정했어요; 4. 헬로우 신문에 있는 프로그램하고 똑같아요; 5. 너무 신나요. 절에서 설 문화를 경험할 수 있고 친구랑 함께 갈 수 있어서요; 6. 절 음식; B) 1. 한국 친척들이 자꾸 "언제 결혼할 거야?" 이런 질문을 해서 스트레스 받아요. 2. 게스트하우스 친구가 "가족이 멀리 있어서 외로워요"라고 말했어요. 그래서 다른 계획을 세우려고 했어요
	Pre-listening activity	여기서부터 저기까지 가요 – 이동하다; 이것을 써요 – 이용하다; 기차,버스, 비행기, 택시, 트램, 지하철 – 대중교통; 여행 가요. 거기서 하룻밤을 자요 – 1박 2일; 여기서 태어나고 자랐어요 – 고향; 50% 보다 많아요 – 반 이상; 이 날은 학교/회사에 안 가요. 집에서 쉬어요 – 연휴
	Listening activity	A) 1, 3, 4; B) 1. 버스를 제일 많이 이용했어요. 그 다음은 기차였어요; 3-1. 18.9%; 3-2. 12.3%

7과	Reading	A) 1. 애기봉 평화 공원 안에 있어요; 2. 북한 마을과 산을 볼 수 있고 커피도 마실 수 있어요. 그리고 북한 사진도 찍을 수 있어요; 3. 젊은 사람들한테 인기가 있어요; 4. 전시관에서 체험 활동도 할 수 있고 전시회도 관람할 수 있어요. 그리고 등산도 할 수 있어요; 5. 〈애기봉 평화 공원〉 웹사이트에서 예약할 수 있어요. 가격은 3,000원이에요. B. 카페에서 북한을 가까이에서 볼 수 있어요/북한이 가까워서 긴장감도 느낄 수 있어요 C) "한국과 북한 사이의 평화를 고민해 볼 수 있어서 여기에 왔어요"라고 말했어요
	After-reading activity	1. 예약번호가 01912345예요; 2. 두 사람이에요. 그래서 티켓 가격은 6,000원이에요; 3. 신분증을 꼭 가지고 가야 해요.
	Listening activity	A) 1, 2; B) 1. (저기) 다리 건너편 위에 있어요; 2. 왼쪽에 있어요; 3. 구경을 다 한 후에 여기에서 다시 셔틀버스를 타야 해요; C) 셔틀버스는 30분마다 와요.

8과	Pre-reading activity	2 – D; 3 – B; 4 – C
	Reading	A) 1. A; 2. L; 3. I; 4. F; 5. G; B) 1. 즉석 떡볶이 냄비에 라면을 넣고 2분만 끓이세요. 그리고 치즈를 넣고 바로 섞으세요. 그리고 볶음밥도 추가해서 먹어야 해요; 2. 로제 떡볶이 2인분, 치즈, 밥; 3. 아니요
	Listening activity	A) 2, 4; B) 1. 떡볶이예요. 떡볶이를 먹어요. 그럼 기분이 좋아요; 2. 자주 먹을 수 있어서요; 3. 집 근처 떡볶이 맛집에 가요. 일주일에 두 번 먹어요; 4. 음식이 빨리 나오고 양도 많아서요; C) 제육볶음 – 맛도 있고 시간도 아낄 수 있어요; 떡볶이 – 스트레스를 풀 수 있어요/기분이 좋아져요

9과	Pre-reading activity	1. 야구장; 2. 팬; 3. 구단; 4. 응원가
	Reading	A) 1, 5; B) 1. 3년 전; 2. 매년 새로운 유니폼을 모아요; 3. 요즘 회사 일이 많아서요; 그리고 티켓을 야구가 인기가 많아서 쉽게 구매할 수 없으니까요; 4. 응원과 야구장 음식이요; 5. 노래방하고 비슷해요; 6. 응원가 연습해요; C) 1. 교통이 복잡하고 지하철을 많이 기다려야 해요; 2. 8회쯤 경기가 끝나기 전에 집에 가요
	Pre-listening activity	어떤 음식을 제일 좋아하세요?; 가장 최근에 어디로 여행을 갔어요?; 어디가 제일 좋았어요?; 시간이 있을 때 보통 뭐 하세요?
	Listening activity	A) 1. 3, 4; B) 1. 쇼핑 앱; 2. 없어요. 나중에 하와이에 여행 가고 싶어해요. 바다를 좋아해서요; 3. 김치찌개; 4. 달리기를 좋아해요. 보통 아침에 일어나서 달리기를 해요; 5. 자기 팀 – 진짜 많은 사람들이 야구 선수들을 좋아하니까 정영수 선수도 야구 선수가 되고 싶어 했어요; 6. "열심히 하고 있으니까 잘봐 주세요! 잘 부탁드리겠습니다"라고 말했어요

10과	Pre-reading activity	1, 2
	Reading	A) 1, 4, 5; B) 1. 해녀들에 대해 이야기 하고 있어요; 2. 아니요. 지금은 해녀 수가 많지 않아요; 3. 11, 520명 적어요; 4. 아니요. 많지 않아요
	Listening activity	A) 1. 2, 5; B) 1. 손으로 해산물을 잡아요; 2. 보통 해산물을 많이 잡지 않고 큰 해산물만 잡아요; 3. 위험하기 때문이에요; C) 나이 많은 해녀와 마음 사람들을 도와줬어요

Appendix 07: Dialogue, Listening Transcripts, and Translations

1과

🎧 대화

사랑: 와, 한복이 많네요!
소피아: 사랑 씨, 우리 먼저 가방을 맡길까요?
사랑: 네, 좋아요! 그런데 어디에 가방을 맡길 수 있어요?
소피아: 지하 보관함에 맡길 수 있어요!
샘: 소피아 씨, 어떻게 이렇게 잘 알아요?
소피아: 아, 구글에서 한복 렌탈을 검색했어요. 거기 리뷰에서 봤어요.

🎧 Conversation

Sarang: Wow, there are so many hanboks!
Sophia: Sarang, shall we leave our bags first?
Sarang: Yes, that's a good idea! But where can we leave our bags?
Sophia: You can leave them in the storage room in the basement!
Sam: Sophia, how did you know that?
Sophia: Oh, I searched for hanbok rentals on Google. I saw it in the reviews.

🎧 듣기

소피아: 안녕하세요? 여러분! 여러분의 여행 친구 소피아예요. 한 달 동안 잘 지내셨어요? 저 다음 주 수요일에 게스트하우스 친구들하고 경복궁에 갈 거예요. 왜냐하면 다음 주부터 프랑스어로 안내를 받을 수 있거든요. 너무 신나요! 참 이번에는 경복궁 근처에서 한복도 빌릴 거예요. 저는 파란색을 좋아해요. 그래서 치마와 저고리 모두 파란색으로 입을 거예요. 여러분! 혹시 그거 아세요? 한복 가게에서 공짜로 한복 머리 스타일링도 받을 수 있어요. 그래서 저는 한복 렌탈 가게에 아침 일찍 갈 거예요. 늦게 가요. 그럼 많이 기다려야 할 거예요. 그리고 늦게 가면 예쁜 옷이 많이 없을 거예요. 그리고 여러분 저는 경복궁에서 유튜브 동영상도 많이 찍을 거예요! 그리고 건축 사진도 많이 찍을 거예요! 여러분 제 경복궁 동영상도 많이 기대해 주세요! 경복궁 동영상은 한 달 뒤에 5월 15일에 업로드할 거예요! 그럼 그 때 만나요!

🎧 Listening activity

Sophia: Hello, everyone! It's Sofia, your travel companion. How have you been for the past month? Next Wednesday, I'm going to Gyeongbok Palace with my friends from the guesthouse. That's because starting next week, I'll be able to get a tour in French. I'm so excited! By the way, this time I'm going to rent a hanbok near Gyeongbok Palace. I like blue, so I'm going to wear a blue skirt and jacket. Did you know that you can get your hair styled for free at hanbok shops? So I'm going to go to the hanbok rental shop early in the morning. Don't go too late. Then I'll have to wait a long time. And if I go late, there won't be many nice outfits left. And everyone, I'm going to take a lot of YouTube videos at Gyeongbok Palace! And I'll take a lot of architectural photos too! Please look forward to my Gyeongbok Palace videos! I'll upload them a month later on 15 May! See you then!

2과

🎧 대화

회사 동료: 우미드, 괜찮아? 무슨 일 있어?
우미드: 아, 응. 좀… 이번 프로젝트 잘 못했어.
회사 동료: 괜찮아. 이번 거 좀 어려웠어?
우미드: 응.
회사 동료: 우미드, 그래도 나보다 잘했잖아.
우미드: 아니야. 그래도 위로 고마워.

🎧 Conversation

Colleague: Umid, are you alright? Is something the matter?
Umid: Oh, yeah. It's just… I didn't do well on this project.
Colleague: It's okay. This one was a bit difficult.
Umid: Yeah.
Colleague: Umid, you still did better than me.
Umid: No, I didn't. But thank you for your encouragement.

🎧 듣기

사랑: 우미드 씨, 요즘 회사 생활은 어때요?
우미드: 괜찮아요. 이제 좀 덜 바빠요. 지난 주에 회사 프로젝트가 하나 끝났어요.
사랑: 아, 그래요? 회사 사람들은 어때요?
우미드: 다 친절해요. 특히 대리님이 진짜 제일 친절하세요. 제가 지난 번에 대리님께 반말했는데 이해해 주셨어요.

🎧 Listening activity

Sarang: Umid, how's work going lately?
Umid: It's okay. It's not as busy now. I wrapped up a project at work last week.
Sarang: Oh, really? How's your team?
Umid: They're all great. Especially my assistant manager. He's really nice. I (accidentally) used casual language with him…, and he totally understood.

사랑: 어떻게 말했는데요?
우미드: 점심 때 "밥 잘 먹었어?" 이렇게 말했어요.
사랑: 아이고~ 그 다음부터는 "식사 잘 하셨어요?" 이렇게 말하세요. 저도 존댓말이 제일 어려워요.
우미드: 사랑 씨도요?
사랑: 네, 아직도 어려워요. 저도 지난번에 비슷한 말실수 했어요. 지난번에 할머니께서 숨비소리 게스트하우스에 오셨어요. 그 때 할머니께 "잘 도착하셨어요?" 이렇게 말했어요.
우미드: 하하하, 할머니께서 괜찮으셨어요?
사랑: 네, 할머니께서도 저를 제일 잘 이해해 주세요. 그래서 할머니를 제일 좋아해요.

Sarang: What did you say?
Umid: At lunchtime, I asked, "Did you eat well?"
Sarang: Oh, from now on, say, "Did you have a good meal?" I also find formal language the toughest.
Umid: You too, Sarang?
Sarang: Yeah, it's still tricky for me. I made a similar mistake last time. An elderly lady came to the guesthouse. I asked her, "Did you arrive safely?"
Umid: Hahaha, was the elderly lady alright?
Sarang: Yes, she gets me the best. That's why I like her the most.

🎧 대화 / 🎧 Conversation

샘: 프리야 씨, 다음 달에 제 친구가 호주에서 와요.
프리야: 와~ 뭐 할 거예요?
샘: 제 친구가 스키를 좋아해요. 그래서 같이 스키장에 갈 거예요. 뭘 준비해야 해요?
프리야: 리프트권을 미리 사야 돼요.
샘: 아 그래요?
프리야: 네. 그런데 스키하고 스키복은 쉽게 빌릴 수 있어요.
샘: 알려 줘서 고마워요. 프리야 씨.

Sam: Priya, my friend is coming from Australia next month.
Priya: Wow, what are you going to do?
Sam: My friend likes skiing, so we're going to go to a ski resort. What should I prepare?
Priya: You should buy lift tickets in advance.
Sam: Oh, really?
Priya: Yes. But you can easily rent skis and ski gear.
Sam: Thanks for letting me know, Priya.

🎧 듣기 전 활동 / 🎧 Pre-listening Activity

1. 샘: 어디에서 스키장 셔틀버스를 타야 해요?
   기차역 매점 아저씨: 역 밖으로 나가세요. 그 다음에 횡단보도를 건너세요. 그럼 축제 포스터가 보일 거예요. 그 앞에서 타세요.
   샘: 감사합니다.

2. 샘 친구: 이 스키장은 뭐가 좋아요?
   프리야: 아. 이 스키장은 셔틀버스가 더 많고 숙박 시설이 좋아요. 그리고 더 싸요.

1. Sam: Where do I catch the ski resort shuttle bus?
   Train station shop owner: Go outside the station. Then cross the pedestrian crossing. You'll see a festival poster. Get on the bus in front of that poster.
   Sam: Thank you.

2. Sam's friend: What's good about this ski resort?
   Priya: Oh, this ski resort has more shuttle buses and the accommodation facilities are good. And it's cheaper.

🎧 듣기 / 🎧 Listening Activity

샘: 프리야, 어디서 셔틀버스를 타야 해? 혹시 알아?
프리야: 나도 잘 모르겠어. 지난 번에는 잠실에서 스키장 버스를 탔어. 그래서 스키장 바로 앞에서 내렸거든.
샘: 아. 괜찮아. 그럼 우리 저기 매점 아주머니께 물어 보자!
프리야: 좋아.

샘: 안녕하세요? 저 혹시 스키장 셔틀버스를 어디에서 타야 해요? 혹시 아세요?
기차역 매점 아주머니: 아, 셔틀버스는 저기 밖에 노란색 포스터 보이세요? 저기로 가세요. 거기로 셔틀버스가 올 거예요.
샘: 네. 감사합니다.

Sam: Priya, where should we catch the shuttle bus? Do you know?
Priya: I'm not sure either. Last time, I took the ski resort bus from Jamsil. So I got off right in front of the ski resort.
Sam: Oh, okay. Let's ask the lady at the snack shop over there!
Priya: Sure.

Sam: Excuse me? Do you know where I can catch the ski resort shuttle bus? Do you happen to know?
Convenience store lady at the train station: Oh, the shuttle bus is over there. Can you see the yellow poster? Go over there. The shuttle bus will come there.
Sam: Okay. Thank you.

샘: 아직 셔틀버스 시간이 남았는데 저기서 기다리자.
샘 친구: 좋아. 근데 이 근처에 다른 스키장도 있어? 헬로우 스키장은 뭐가 좋아?
샘: 어. 헬로우 스키장은 다른 스키장보다 셔틀버스가 많아. 그리고 숙박 시설도 넓고 깨끗해. 게다가 숙박 가격은 다른 곳 보다 싸.
프리야 & 샘 친구: 어~ 셔틀버스 왔다! 얼른 타자!

Sam: There's still time before the shuttle bus arrives. Let's wait there.
Sam's friend: Alright. By the way, are there any other ski resorts around here? What's good about Hello Ski Resort?
Sam: Yeah. Hello Ski Resort has more shuttle buses than other ski resorts. Plus, the accommodation facilities are spacious and clean. And the accommodation prices are cheaper than other places.
Priya & Sam's friend: Oh, the shuttle bus is here! Let's hurry up and get on!

4과

🎧 대화 / 🎧 Conversation

안내 직원: 어서 오세요. 반갑습니다. 티켓 확인 도와드리겠습니다.
하루: 네? 다시 한번 말씀해 주세요.
안내 직원: 아, 티켓 확인을 도와드리겠습니다.
하루: 네! 여기 있습니다.
안내 직원: 여기 이 클래퍼도 가져 가십시오.
하루: 네. 감사합니다. 그런데 저 혹시 R석은 어느 쪽으로 가야 해요?
안내 직원: R석은 저쪽입니다.
하루: 감사합니다.

Information staff: Welcome. Nice to meet you. Let me check your tickets.
Haru: Yes? Could you repeat that?
Information desk staff: Oh, I'll help you check your ticket.
Haru: Yes! Here it is.
Information desk staff: Here, please take this clapper (a cheering stick that makes a clapping sound) as well.
Haru: Yes, thank you. By the way, which way should I go to get to the R seats?
Information desk staff: The R seats are over there.
Haru: Thank you.

🎧 듣기 전 활동 / 🎧 Pre-listening Activity

이 버스는 경기도 버스입니다.
안전벨트를 해 주십시오.

동영상을 찍을 수 없습니다.
그리고 동영상을 *SNS에 업로드하실 수 없습니다.

이번 역은 강남역입니다.
내리실 문은 오른쪽입니다.

This is a Gyeonggi-do bus.
Please fasten your seatbelts.

You cannot take videos.
And you cannot upload videos to social media.

This is Gangnam Station.
The exit door is on the right.

🎧 듣기 / 🎧 Listening Activity

캐롤라인: 안녕하세요?
하루 어머니: 안녕하세요? 저는 하루 엄마예요. 게이코 아라이예요. 하루가 이 가수를 좋아해요. 그래서 같이 왔어요. 그런데 저는 한국어를 잘 못해요.
캐롤라인: 아니에요. 잘하시는데요? 저도 미국에서 딸이 한국에 놀러 왔어요. 그래서 같이 공연 보러 왔어요. 그런데 하루는 어디에 갔어요?
하루 어머니: 방금 화장실에 갔어요.
📢 안내원: 공연 중에 휴대 전화로 사진이나 동영상을 찍을 수 없습니다. 그리고 음식을 드실 수 없습니다. 감사합니다.
하루 어머니: 무슨 이야기예요?
캐롤라인: 아, 콘서트 중에는 사진을 찍을 수 없어요. 그리고 음식도 먹을 수 없어요.
하루 어머니: 알려줘서 고마워요.
캐롤라인: 그런데 그건 뭐예요?
하루 어머니: 이건 응원봉이에요. 하루 거예요. 하루 보물 1호예요.
캐롤라인: 응원봉이 예뻐요!

Caroline: Hello?
Haru's mother: Hello? I'm Haru's mother. My name is Keiko Arai. Haru likes this singer, so I came with her. But I don't speak Korean very well.
Caroline: No, you do. I have a daughter who came to Korea from the United States, so I came to see the performance with her. Where is Haru?
Haru's mother: She just went to the restroom.
📢 Announcement: During the performance, you may not take photos or videos with your mobile phones. And you may not eat any food. Thank you.
Haru's mother: What's that about?
Caroline: Oh, you can't take photos during the concert. And you can't eat either.
Haru's mother: Thank you for letting me know.
Caroline: What's that?
Haru's mother: This is a cheer stick. It's Haru's. It's her number one treasure.
Caroline: The cheer stick is so cute!

🎧 활동

(버스 안내 방송) [listening 4.4]
이 버스는 경기도 버스입니다. 안전벨트를 해 주십시오.

(영화관 안내 방송) [listening 4.5]
영화관에서는 동영상을 찍을 수 없습니다.
그리고 동영상을 개인 소셜 미디어에 업로드할 수 없습니다.

(지하철 안내 방송) [listening 4.6]
이번 역은 강남역입니다. 내리실 문은 오른쪽입니다.
출입문 닫습니다. 출입문 닫습니다.

🎧 (After-listening) Activity

(Bus announcement) [listening 4.4]
This bus is a Gyeonggi-do bus. Please fasten your seat belt.

(Cinema announcement) [LISTENING 4.5]
You are not allowed to take videos in the cinema, and you are not allowed to upload videos to your personal social media.

(Subway announcement) [LISTENING 4.6]
This is Gangnam Station. The exit door is on the right. Please close the door. Please close the door.

🎧 대화

마두카: 안녕하세요?
병원 직원: 안녕하세요? 예약하셨어요?
마두카: 아니요. 예약 안 했어요. 처음 왔어요.
병원 직원: 그럼 이거 한 장 써 주세요.
마두카: 네. 알겠습니다.
...
병원 직원: 마두카 씨, 이쪽으로 오세요.
의사: 어디가 불편하세요?
마두카: 넘어져서 무릎을 다쳤어요.

🎧 Conversation

Maduka: Hello?
Hospital staff: Hello, do you have an appointment?
Maduka: No, I don't have an appointment. I'm new here.
Hospital staff: Then can you fill this out?
Maduka: Yes. Okay.
...
Hospital staff: Maduka, please come this way.
Doctor: In which areas do you experience discomfort?
Maduka: I fell and hurt my knee.

🎧 듣기

사랑: 저, 배가 너무 아프고 열이 많이 나서요.
의사: 네. 언제부터 아팠어요?
사랑: 지난주 주말부터 배가 아팠어요. 배가 아파서 밤에 잠도 잘 못잤어요.
의사: 배는 몇 시간 동안 아팠어요? 계속 아팠어요?
사랑: 음… 밥을 먹은 후에 더 아팠고 30분 동안 계속 아팠어요.

의사: 그래서 어떻게 했어요?
사랑: 소화제를 먹었어요. 그리고 소화제를 먹은 후에 잠을 많이 잤어요.
의사: 괜찮았어요?
사랑: 네. 조금 괜찮았어요. 그런데 어제부터는 열도 났어요. 그런데 주말이어서 병원에 못 왔어요.
의사: 네. 혹시 가족들도 아프세요?
사랑: 아니요. 가족들은 영국에 있어요. 지난주에 부모님을 만나러 영국에 갔다 왔어요.
의사: 아, 네. 장염이에요. 그럼 약을 처방해 줄게요. 그리고 물을 많이 드시고 오늘은 식사하지 마세요. 그리고 내일부터는 부드러운 죽을 드세요. 계속 아프면 병원에 꼭 다시 오세요.

🎧 Listening activity

Sarang: I have a terrible stomach ache and a high fever.
Doctor: Okay. When did it start?
Sarang: It started last weekend. The pain was so bad that I couldn't sleep well at night.
Doctor: How long has the pain been going on? Has it been constant?
Sarang: Um... It got worse after I ate, and it lasted for about half an hour.

Doctor: What did you do?
Sarang: I took some antacids. And after taking the antacids, I slept a lot.
Doctor: Did you feel better?
Sarang: Yes, I felt a little better. But then I started running a fever yesterday. But since it was the weekend, I couldn't come to the hospital.
Doctor: Okay. Are any of your family members sick?
Sarang: No. My family is in England. I went to England last week to visit my parents.
Doctor: Oh, okay. It's gastroenteritis. I'll prescribe some medication. Drink plenty of water and don't eat anything today. Starting tomorrow, eat only soft porridge. If you continue to feel unwell, please come back to the hospital immediately.

6과

🎧 대화

캐롤라인: 사랑 씨는 이번 설 연휴에 뭐 할 거예요?
사랑: 이번에는 제주도 할머니 댁에 가요.
거기서 차례를 지내려고 해요. 캐롤라인 씨는요?
캐롤라인: 저는 아직 계획이 없어요.
사랑: 그럼 제주도 할머니 댁에 같이 가실래요?
제가 할머니한테 물어볼게요.
캐롤라인: 네, 좋아요.

🎧 Conversation

Caroline: What are you doing for the Lunar New Year holiday?
Sarang: This time, I'm heading to my grandmother's house on Jeju Island. I'll be enjoying a holiday ritual there. What about you?
Caroline: I don't have any plans yet.
Sarang: Then, would you like to join me at my grandmother's house on Jeju Island? I'll ask my grandmother.
Caroline: Yeah, that sounds lovely.

🎧 듣기

[앵커] 올 설 연휴에는 작년보다 많은 사람들이 이동했습니다.

김철수 기자가 설명해 드리겠습니다.

[기자]
네. 이번 연휴는 1월 27일부터 30일까지였습니다. 올해 설 연휴에는 총 3482만 명이 이동했습니다. 거의 대한민국 인구의 52%의 사람들이 고향으로 갔습니다. 교통수단으로 개인 자동차가 85.7%로 제일 많았습니다. 대중교통 중에서는 버스가 5.3%로 사람들이 제일 많이 이용했습니다. 그 다음으로는 기차가 4.2%였습니다.
서울-부산 사이는 자동차로 6시간 51분 정도 걸렸습니다.
서울 강릉은 4시간 18분 정도 걸렸습니다.
올해 설 연휴 동안에는 가장 많은 사람들이 '2박 3일' 동안 고향에서 지냈습니다. 그 다음으로 많은 사람들이 '1박 2일' 동안 고향에 있었습니다.
설 연휴 동안에 18.9%의 사람들은 여행을 갔다왔습니다. 그 중에서 12.3%는 해외로 여행을 갔습니다.

헬로우 뉴스 김철수입니다.

🎧 Listening activity

[Anchor] More people travelled during this year's Lunar New Year holiday than last year.

Reporter Kim Cheol-soo has more.

[Reporter]
Yep. The holiday period ran from the 27th to the 30th of January. A total of 34.82 million people travelled during this year's Lunar New Year holiday. This accounts for nearly 52% of South Korea's population returning to their hometowns. Private cars represented 85.7% of all transportation, making them the most popular mode of travel. Among public transportation options, buses were the most commonly used at 5.3%, followed by trains at 4.2%.
The journey from Seoul to Busan took about 6 hours and 51 minutes by car. The trip from Seoul to Gangneung took around 4 hours and 18 minutes.
During this year's Lunar New Year holiday, the largest number of people spent '2 nights and 3 days' in their hometowns, while the next largest group spent '1 night and 2 days'.
During the Lunar New Year holiday, 18.9% of people went on trips, with 12.3% travelling overseas.

Hello News, Kim Cheol-soo.

7과

🎧 대화

마두카: 이 카페 사진 봤어요? 북한에서 가까운 곳에 카페가 생겼어요. 카페에서 북한이 보여요.
가브리엘: 아니요. 못 봤어요. 서울에서 가까워요?
마두카: 네. 서울에서 갈 수 있어요.
가브리엘: 그런데 대중교통으로 갈 수 있을까요?
마두카: 네. 갈 수 있어요! 그런데 시간이 좀 걸려요.

🎧 Conversation

Maduka: Have you seen the photo of this café? A café has opened near North Korea, and you can see North Korea from the café.
Gabriel: No, I haven't seen it. Is it close to Seoul?
Maduka: Yes, you can get there from Seoul.
Gabriel: But can you reach it by public transport?
Maduka: Yes, you can! But it takes a bit of time.

🎧 듣기

가브리엘: 안녕하세요? 저 온라인으로 예약을 했는데요.
매표소 직원: 신분증 가지고 오셨죠?
가브리엘: 네, 여기 있어요.

🎧 Listening activity

Gabriel: Hello? I made a reservation online.
Ticket office employee: Do you have your ID with you?
Gabriel: Yes, here it is.

매표소 직원: 여기 티켓이고요. 이따가 셔틀버스를 탄 다음에 티켓을 검사할 거예요. 그리고 셔틀버스는 왼쪽 주차장에서 탈 수 있어요.
가브리엘: 네, 감사합니다.

마두카: 셔틀버스가 언제 올까요?
가브리엘: 저 안내 아저씨한테 물어 볼게요. 저, 죄송한데요. 셔틀버스가 언제 올까요?
안내원: 30분쯤 뒤에 올 거예요.
가브리엘: 공원 안에 개인 자동차로도 갈 수 있을까요?
안내원: 네. 개인 자동차로도 갈 수 있고 셔틀버스로도 갈 수 있어요. 아, 저기 버스 왔어요.

운전 기사님: 다 왔습니다. 공원 카페는 저기 다리 건너편 위에 있어요. 그리고 공원 전시관은 왼쪽에 있어요. 다 구경한 다음에 여기서 다시 셔틀버스를 타세요. 셔틀버스는 30분마다 와요.
가브리엘/마두카: 네. 감사합니다. 기사님.

Ticket office employee: Here's your ticket. We'll check it after you board the shuttle bus. The shuttle bus departs from the parking lot on the left.
Gabriel: Okay, thank you.

Maduka: When will the shuttle bus arrive?
Gabriel: I'll ask the attendant. Excuse me, when will the shuttle bus arrive?
Attendant: It will arrive in about 30 minutes.
Gabriel: Can I go to the park by private car?
Guide: Yeah, you can go by private car or by shuttle bus. Oh, here comes the bus.

Driver: We're here. The park café is across the bridge and up ahead. The park exhibition hall is on the left. After you've finished exploring, take the shuttle bus back here. The shuttle bus comes every 30 minutes.
Gabriel/Maduka: Okay. Thank you, driver.

8과

🎧 대화

마두카: 무슨 떡볶이 영상이야?
타오: 즉석 떡볶이 맛집이야.
마두카: 와, 맛있겠다! 다른 즉석 떡볶이랑 좀 달라?
타오: 응. 여기는 떡볶이에 토마토 소스하고 치즈를 넣어.
마두카: 그렇구나. 우리 저기 가서 다 같이 먹어 보자!
타오: 좋은 생각이야!

🎧 Conversation

Maduka: What kind of tteokbokki video is that?
Tao: It's a famous spot for instant tteokbokki.
Maduka: Wow, that looks delicious! Is it different from other instant tteokbokki?
Tao: Yeah. They add tomato sauce and cheese to the tteokbokki here.
Maduka: I see. Let's go there and try it together!
Tao: Great idea!

🎧 듣기

MC 나리: 안녕하세요? "맛집 투어" 팟캐스트 MC 나리입니다. 저는 요즘에 맛집 책을 쓰고 있어서 지난 한 달 동안 좀 바빴어요. 그래서 요즘 좀 많이 피곤해요. 여러분들도 요즘 혹시 힘들거나 피곤하세요? 그럼 이 때 무슨 음식을 드세요? 저는 떡볶이를 먹어요. 그럼 기분이 좋아요. 떡볶이는 제 소울 푸드예요.

이번 시간에는 여러분들과 소울 푸드 이야기를 하려고 해요. 한국인의 소울 푸드는 무엇일까요? 한국인의 소울 푸드 순위를 1위부터 3위까지 정리했어요.

3위는 김치찌개예요. 왜냐하면 김치찌개는 자주 먹을 수 있어서요. 생각보다 많은 사람들이 김치찌개를 좋아해요.

2위는 떡볶이예요. 저도 초등학교 때부터 떡볶이를 아주 좋아했어요. 요즘도 일주일에 두 번은 집 근처 떡볶이 맛집에 가서 먹어요.

그리고 두구두구두구 1위는 제육볶음이에요! 특히 점심 때 회사원들이 제육볶음을 가장 많이 주문해요. 왜냐하면 음식이 빨리 나오고 양도 많아서요.

여러분들도 시간이 없어서 점심을 빨리 먹어야 해요? 그럼 제육볶음을 추천해요! 맛도 있고 시간도 아낄 수 있어요! 스트레스가 많아요? 그럼 떡볶이를 추천해요! 스트레스를 풀 수 있어요!

🎧 Listening activity

MC Nari: Hello, everyone! This is Nari, host of the 'Foodie Tour' podcast. I've been busy writing a book about delicious restaurants, so I've been quite busy for the past month. That's why I've been feeling a bit tired lately. Are any of you feeling tired or stressed these days? What do you eat when you feel that way? I eat tteokbokki. It makes me feel better. Tteokbokki is my soul food.

This time, I want to chat about soul food with you. What is the soul food of Koreans? I've ranked the soul foods of Koreans from 1st to 3rd place.

Third place goes to kimchi stew. You can eat it often, and more people enjoy kimchi stew than you might think.

Second place is tteokbokki. I've loved tteokbokki since my primary school days. Even now, I visit a tteokbokki restaurant near my place twice a week.

And drumroll, drumroll, drumroll... the number one is jeyuk bokkeum! Especially at lunchtime, office workers order jeyuk bokkeum the most. Why? Because it comes out quickly and the portions are generous.

Do you also need to grab lunch quickly because you're short on time? Then I recommend jeyuk bokkeum! It's delicious and saves time! Feeling stressed? Then I recommend tteokbokki! You can ease stress!

🎧 대화	🎧 Conversation
타오: 반 빈 씨 야구 좋아해요? 반 빈: 네! 타오: 이번 주말에 샘하고 같이 야구 보러 가려고 해요. 같이 가실래요? 반 빈: 오, 좋아요. 어느 야구장으로 갈 거예요? 타오: 아직 안 정했어요. 서울 팀 야구장이 가까우니까 여기 어때요? 반 빈: 그래요! 타오: 그리고 야구장에 맛있는 음식을 많이 파니까 저녁은 거기 가서 먹어요!	Tao: Van Binh, do you like baseball? Van Binh: Yes! Tao: I'm planning to go watch a baseball game with Sam this weekend. Would you like to join us? Van Binh: Oh, that sounds great! Which stadium are you going to? Tao: I haven't decided yet. The Seoul team's stadium is nearby, so how about there? Van Binh: Sure! Tao: And there's plenty of good food at the stadium, so let's have dinner there!
🎧 듣기	🎧 Listening activity
기자 Q: 정영수 선수, 준비되셨죠? 그럼 50문 50답 시작하겠습니다. 정영수 A: 네! Q: 이름? A: 정영수입니다. Q: 생년월일? A: 2001년 10월 10일입니다. Q: 성격 장점은? A: 긍정적이에요. 그리고 친한 사람들하고 이야기도 많이 해요. Q: 단점은? A: 쉽게 친구를 못 사귑니다. Q: 보물 1호는? A: 가족입니다. Q: 프로필 사진은? A: 대만에 가서 이 사진을 찍었습니다. Q: 어떤 앱을 자주 쓰세요? A: 쇼핑 앱을 많이 씁니다. Q: 매일 먹을 수 있는 음식은? A: 김치찌개요. 매운 음식이요. Q: 어떤 여행이 가장 기억나세요? A: 아직 없어요. 나중에 하와이에 가고 싶습니다. 제가 바다를 좋아 해서요. Q: 수영 잘 하세요? A: 네. 잘합니다. Q: 휴일에 뭐 하세요? A: 보통 잠을 많이 잡니다. 12시간 잡니다. Q: 다른 스포츠 중에서 뭘 좋아하세요? A: 달리기를 좋아합니다. 아침에 일어나서 1시간 정도 가까운 공원에서 달립니다. Q: 어느 야구팀을 제일 좋아하세요?: A: 당연히 저희 팀이죠!! 10살 때 처음 아버지랑 이 경기장에 왔어요. 진짜 많은 사람들이 야구 선수들을 좋아하니까 저도 야구 선수가 되고 싶었습니다. Q: 팬들에게 한 마디? A: 열심히 하고 있으니까 잘 봐 주세요!! 잘 부탁드리겠습니다. Q: 오늘 인터뷰 감사합니다! A: 네. 고맙습니다.	Reporter Q: Jeong Young-soo, are you ready? Let's kick off with 50 questions and 50 answers. Jeong Young-soo A: Yes! Q: What's your name? A: My name is Jeong Young-soo. Q: When's your birthday? A: I was born on 10 October 2001. Q: What are your strengths? A: I'm a positive person and I often chat a lot with my close friends. Q: What are your weaknesses? A: I find it a bit challenging to make friends easily. Q: What's your most prized possession? A: My family. Q: What's your profile picture? A: I took this photo in Taiwan. Q: Which apps do you use often? A: I frequently use shopping apps. Q: What food could you eat every day? A: Kimchi stew. Spicy food. Q: What's your most memorable trip? A: Not yet. I want to go to Hawaii someday because I love the ocean. Q: Are you a good swimmer? A: Yes, I do. Q: What do you do on your days off? A: I usually sleep a fair bit. About 12 hours. Q: What other sports do you enjoy? A: I enjoy running. I wake up in the morning and run for about an hour at a nearby park. Q: Which baseball team do you support the most? A: Of course, it's our team!! When I was 10, I first came to this stadium with my father. Since so many people love baseball players, I wanted to become one too. Q: Any message for your fans? A: I'm working hard, so please keep an eye on me!! Q: Thanks for the interview today! A: Please look

10과

🎧 대화

선덕 할머니: 바다까지 왜 나왔어? 집에서 기다리지?
사랑: 캐롤라인 씨가 해녀에 관심이 많아서 할머니 보러 같이 왔어요.
캐롤라인: 안녕하세요?
선덕 할머니: 그래요. 잘 왔어요.
캐롤라인: 어… 할머님, 해녀 일이 힘들지 않으세요?
선덕 할머니: 아니요. 즐거워요.

🎧 Conversation

Grandma Seon-deok: Why did you come all the way to thesea? Why didn't you wait at home?
Sarang: Ms. Caroline is really interested in female divers, so she came with me to see you.
Caroline: Hello.
Grandma Seon-deok: Yes. Welcome.
Caroline: Um… Grandma, isn't the work of a female diver tough?
Grandma Seon-deok: No, it's enjoyable.

🎧 듣기

강연자: 안녕하세요? 지금부터 해녀 박물관 강연 시리즈 수업을 시작하겠습니다. 오늘 강연을 들으러 와 주셔서 감사합니다. 여러분 한국에서 최초의 여성 직업은 무엇이었을까요?
캐롤라인: 해녀요!
강연자: 네. 맞습니다. 해녀 직업은 오래전부터 있었습니다. 해녀들은 바다에 들어가서 해산물을 잡아서 팔았습니다. 해녀들은 열심히 일해서 가족들과 마을 사람들을 도와줬어요. 해녀들은 7살에서 8살때부터 가까운 바다에서 해녀 일을 배우고 연습해요. 그리고 18살쯤부터는 바다에 들어가서 일할 수 있어요.
캐롤라인: 선생님, 해녀들은 어떻게 해산물을 잡아요?
강연자: 손으로 해산물을 잡아요.
캐롤라인: 해산물을 많이 잡을 수 있어요?
강연자: 네. 그런데 보통 해산물을 많이 잡지 않고 큰 해산물만 잡아요. 왜냐하면 자연을 지키고 싶어서요.
캐롤라인: 해녀들은 어떻게 일을 해요?
강연자: 해녀 일은 혼자서 하지 못합니다. 위험하기 때문이에요. 그래서 해녀들은 바다에 들어가기 전에 다 같이 준비하고 바다에서 함께 일합니다. 그리고 해녀들은 일을 한 후에 돈도 함께 나누었어요.
캐롤라인: 왜 돈을 같이 나눴어요?
강연자: 나이 많은 해녀와 마을 사람을 도와주려고요. 혹시 다른 질문 있으세요?

🎧 Listening activity

Lecturer: Hello, everyone. We'll now kick off the lecture series at the Haenyeo Museum. Thanks for coming to listen to today's talk. What do you reckon was the first female occupation in Korea?
Caroline: Haenyeo!
Lecturer: That's right. The haenyeo profession has been around for a long time. Haenyeo dive into the sea to catch seafood and sell it. They've worked hard to support their families and the people in their villages. Haenyeo start learning and practising the trade in nearby seas from about the age of 7 or 8. By the time they're around 18, they can begin working in the sea.
Caroline: Teacher, how do haenyeo catch seafood?
Lecturer: They catch seafood with their hands.
Caroline: Can they catch a lot of seafood?
Lecturer: Yeah, but they usually don't catch a lot; they only catch larger seafood. This is to protect nature.
Caroline: How do haenyeo work?
Lecturer: Haenyeo work cannot be done alone because it's dangerous. So, before entering the sea, they prepare together and work as a team in the water. After they finish, they also share the earnings.
Caroline: Why do they share the money?
Lecturer: To support older haenyeo and locals. Do you have any other questions?

ANNYEONG? KOREAN! _ Volume 2

초판인쇄	2025년 06월 27일
초판발행	2025년 07월 03일

지 은 이	김현미(Hyun Mi Kim), 조지은(Jieun Kiaer), 니콜라 프라스키니(Nicola Fraschini)
펴 낸 이	허대우
마 케 팅	황현경
편집 및 디자인	이승미
캐릭터 디자인	이재엽
펴 낸 곳	주식회사 헬로우코리안
주 소	경기도 고양시 덕양구 향동로 217, 10층 KA1014호
문 의	hello@hellokorean.co.kr
출판신고	2024년 6월 28일 제395-2024-000141호
인 쇄	헬로우프린텍

이 책은 저작권법에 따라 보호받는 저작물이므로 무단전재와 무단복제를 금하며,
이 책 내용의 전부 또는 일부를 이용하려면 반드시 저작권자와 헬로우코리안의 서면 동의를 받아야 합니다.